LEADERSHIP CANDY

18 MANAGEMENT ESSENTIALS EVERY RISING LEADER SHOULD KNOW

Charles Manning

Contact: info@beapowerleader.com

1st Edition

ISBN 978-0-692-15207-2

Contents

Introduction

LEADERSHIP CANDY is the companion handbook to the popular seminar series "*Management Essentials for Rising Leaders*", a fun and interactive seminar that strengthens existing leaders, and prepares rising leaders to take on new leadership roles.

So what's the 'Candy' about? The key theme in this handbook is that leadership skills alone are not enough for a rising leader to be successful. A leader also needs specific management skills.

LEADERSHIP SKILLS ALONE ARE NOT ENOUGH. A LEADER ALSO NEEDS SPECIFIC MANAGEMENT SKILLS

The 18 management skills presented here are the candy (the tasty morsels) that a leader consumes to sweeten their leadership effectiveness and transform them from an average leader into a Power Leader.

I had considered a title with some cool name that communicates that management skills are the *Spice* that flavors leadership effectiveness; and that without these management spices, a leader is flavorless; but in the end *Candy* won out.

LEADERSHIP CANDY will empower the:

MANAGER - To quickly equip managers with best-of-the-best management skills taught in top business schools, to prepare them to take on leadership roles

EXECUTIVE - To help executives develop their workforce to become more effective, and deliver professional, high quality results

ORGANIZATION - To help diagnose programs and projects, then supercharge them to deliver outstanding results

BONUS chapter: "YOUR FIRST 30 DAYS" - will guide leaders along a proven four phase model, so they can take on a new leadership role with confidence!

The essential management tools and techniques presented here are the *best-of-the-best.* They can be used independently, and in any order, or they can be combined to deliver outstanding results. We'll explain each one independently; then for the capstone project (the Organizational Assessment), we'll help you make sense of how they could be used together.

The Power Leader can apply these tools and techniques to any job industry. For the government leader, this handbook offers a chapter specific to application in the government arena; and delivers case study examples reflective of problem sets experienced by many government administrators.

HANDBOOK STRUCTURE

The first part of this handbook offers context for which to understand and apply the tools and techniques you are about to learn. Remember that *management* is a different skill-set than *leadership*, so keep the below thoughts in mind as you learn, explore, and practice the upcoming management tools and techniques. Understanding the context of why you use a tool, and how to optimize its potential, will significantly increase your effectiveness!

The second part of this guidebook introduces you to the essential management tools and techniques that Power Leaders use. For each tool, we- define it, describe how it's used, describe what bad things can happen if you don't use it, give an example of its use, and offer a template for you to apply it to your own challenges.

Good luck!

SEMINAR SERIES

Be sure to host or attend the popular LEADERSHIP CANDY "Management Essentials for Rising Leaders" seminar and learn the essential management tools and techniques showcased in this book!

To host or attend a seminar, visit www.beapowerleader.com.

PART I

CONTEXT

LEADERSHIP CANDY

Management vs Leadership

Chapter 1

This handbook transformed the rising leader into a Power Leader by quickly equipping him/her with the essential management skills they need to be successful and stand out from their peers.

Objectives	**Terms**
When you complete Chapter 1, you will be able to: • Describe 6 ways management is different than leadership • Describe why both leadership and management skills are required for success	• Leadership • Management • Organizational Transformation • Change Management

So, let's be clear- management is not the same as leadership. Sure, there are overlaps, but leaders focus on 'what to do', while managers focus on the 'how to do it'.

MANAGEMENT IS NOT THE SAME AS LEADERSHIP

The leader serves as a visionary, and world-class communicator. She charts the course for her organization, shares her vision, and inspires others to participate. She's the person on the stage announcing a great new idea, and paints an empowering picture of where the organization is going.

But once the visionary is done with her speech, how does her vision get implemented on time, on budget, on scope, and with employee buy-in and support? Answer – superior management skills.

The manager implements the leader's vision. He orchestrates the steps and processes that people perform to make the leader's vision a reality. Learning these essential management skills that compliment leadership skills is what this handbook is about.

Leaders Focus On	Managers Focus On
Vision	Goals & objectives
Selling what and why	Telling how and when
People	Design & structure
Innovating	Administrating
Inspiring trust	Directing & Controlling
Policy	Procedures
"Good leaders do the right thing" (what to do)	"Good managers do the thing right" (how best to do it)

Table 1.1 – Leadership vs Management

To clarify, good leaders follow widely recognized tactics such as:

- Praise in public , discipline in private
- Serve others first (food, equipment, benefits...)
- Give credit to others for successes, and take blame for failures
- Etc. More on this later...

But, leadership skills alone are not enough to successfully run an organization. For an organization or project to succeed, every-day leaders must become Power Leaders, and apply essential management skills too.

BOTH LEADERSHIP SKILLS AND MANAGEMENT SKILLS ARE REQUIRED TO SUCCESSFULLY RUN AN ORGANIZATION

These skills you're about to learn have mystifying 'consultant-speak' names, but that's so consultants can charge more for their services (just kidding!). Actually, they're really quite simple to understand. Here, I'll prove it to you now.

FANCY TERM	SIMPLE MEANING
Strategic Planning	What a power leader's gonna do, and how they're gonna do it
Organizational Transformation	Change how your organization operates
Process Mapping	The steps involved in doing a job
Strategic Communications	Getting the message out and gaining worker buy-in
Change Management	Keeping people calm and gaining worker buy-in
Performance Metrics	Measuring the stuff you do
Dashboards	Status reporting
S.W.A.T. Analysis	A quick summary of what's good, what's bad
Baseline	How do we do this now
Control Charts	How we know if things are going good or bad
Decision-matrix analysis	What's the best option
Out of the Box Thinking	Please don't make me explain this...

Table 1.2- Consultant Terms

See, I told you it was easy!

Government Edition

Chapter 2

Okay, so we said this is the 'Government Edition', so here's what a Power Leader needs to understand.

Objectives When you complete Chapter 2, you will be able to: • Describe six issues that make government leadership and management different than private sector leadership and management	**Terms** • Group Think • Veil of Ignorance

SPEND YOUR ENTIRE BUDGET

Meeting public expectation for services is king; therefore you're expected to spend your entire budget to best meet public expectations (without going over of course). Yes, government is into efficiency and cost savings, but not at the expense of failing to deliver services. This is why government organizations always seek to spend their entire budget, and not to reserve some for later. Government's goal is to deliver the best program outcome for the public interest, in the most financially responsible manner.

Author's Note: While spending money to best serve the public interest is good. I argue that public governance has an obligation to operate more efficiently. But, without the requirement to operate more efficiently, what's the incentive to do so? Perhaps together we can initiate this change by implementing efficiency metrics in our operations.

PUBLIC ACCOUNTABILITY & TRANSPARENCY

Another difference that sets government apart from the private sector and non-profit organizations, is that Government has a higher level of accountability and transparency to the general public. Non-profits are accountable to its board of directors (a small group); the private sector is accountable to its shareholders (a mid-size group), and government is accountable to the largest base of people- tax-payers! Thus the greater need to be transparent to the masses.

Because of a higher level of transparency, as a government employee you gotta (yes, 'gotta' is a real word) consider the public perception of your actions and decisions, even if the actions are totally legitimate. For example, when you send your team members to training classes and conferences, think about how the public will view their Las Vegas conference location when it ends up on social media sites and online newspaper comment sections. Maybe the comments will be good, or maybe bad. As an alternative and more publicly acceptable solution, consider an equally competent training conference at a less glamorous location. Just a thought.

Also, keep in the back of your mind how the impact of the Freedom of Information Act (FOIA) will affect how you communicate. Under few exceptions, you should know that your emails, reports and documents are open to public view upon request. Now think back to some 'interesting' emails you sent. Could they become 'embarassing' when open to public view? Yikes!

GOVERNMENT IS GENERALLY RISK AVERSE

Unlike Apple or Sony, there is very little gain for the government to take risks, even smart risks. Think about it, what's the benefit to government to start a new risky program or service, such as a jobs program, or drug rehabilitation program?

Think about the many studies and rounds of discussion that government performs before they make even the smallest decision. For example, replacing a stop sign with a traffic light; consider the archeological, agricultural, and animal studies to be conducted before building it, or a roadway or building a bridge.

The attention paid to 'unintended consequences' (unforeseen risk) is a key reason why government goes slooooow and in incremental steps. For example, minimum wage laws intended to help increase salary for low-skill workers can unintentionally create unemployment (unintended consequence), because the employer may not be able to afford to keep the employee hired, or hired at a full-time status. Government administration can be tricky.

So what's the incentive for taking risk? Does the government earn more profit if they start a new program? No. However if the risky program fails, the potential downside is for substantial public criticism and possibly loss of the administrator's job. Yikes again!

So what's a Power Leader to do? Answer-

- Consider and investigate multiple dimensions of the issue (without paralysis by analysis), and
- Conduct contingency planning, to account for the "what-ifs" that could emerge, and
- Embrace the concept of incremental improvement. Baby steps.

SETTING A PRECEDENT

When a Power Leader makes decisions, he smartly makes his decision based on what he would do, not only for the current circumstance, but for the next and all future incidents of this same type. For example, if one of your team members asks you if they can work from home one day a week. You might be tempted to say 'yes'. But, before you respond, ask yourself what if other team members learn of this and also ask to work from home? I guess what I'm saying is, is before you act, play a movie in your head of how this and the next incident will play out. Then, armed with this 'movie', make your decision.

VEIL OF IGNORANCE

This is one of my favorite and useful tools to help make effective decisions. First introduced in 1971 by philosopher John Rawls, the veil of ignorance describes how to make unbiased decisions. Basically, it says to make your decision assuming that you don't know yet which social group will be affected.

For example, do you set a city policy to prevent homes from renting out spare basement bedrooms? If you don't rent out your own basement, then perhaps you might choose to implement the policy. However, if your mother rents out her basement room as her only source of retirement income, then you might be tempted to refute the policy. Rawls says that we should make our decisions not knowing which social group will benefit or be harmed? The veil allows us to reason objectively about what a fair society looks like.

Others describe the veil of ignorance with an analogy that I find kinda funny. It goes like this- Suppose there's one last piece of cake to share between you and a friend, while *you* get to cut the last piece in half, the *other person* gets to choose the first piece! (Explanation: if you cut the last piece of cake into a large piece and smaller piece, the other person might choose the larger piece. So, to avoid getting a smaller piece, you try to cut the piece as even (fair) as possible. Did I really have to explain that?)

AVOID GROUP-THINK

Group-think is about 'yes-men'. Group think happens when people in a meeting all agree to a clearly dysfunctional solution, rather than disagree and stand out as the lone outcast or dissenter. Teams suffer from group-think when they desire harmony in the group over wisdom, even though the result is an irrational or foolish decision-making outcome. To avoid group-think and make better decisions, a

Power Leader creates a culture where alternate/conflicting points of view are valued and without repercussion.

Here's a way to avoid group-think: appoint someone in the working group to serve the role of "devil's advocate"- responsible to point out alternative viewpoints, and express the negative consequences of the decision option. By assigning this role, it takes away the guilt and fear factor of non-conformity. The result is a better decision-making outcome. And by the way, for each meeting, don't assign the same person as the devil's advocate, spread the 'honor' around to others.

Challenges of Your New Role

Chapter 3

Now that you're in a position of responsibility and leadership, some of your office behaviors and choices have to change. By now, they should already have changed!

Objectives When you complete Chapter 3, you will be able to: • Describe two solutions to the challenges of taking on a new leadership role • Describe four solutions to build team trust	**Terms** • Forming, Storming, Norming, and Performing model • Ground Truth • Stand-up meeting

FEARS OF TAKING ON A NEW ROLE

First thing, take a deep breath- you can do this. Likely, you feel as if you're in foreign territory, pushed out of your comfort zone, and wonder if you can actually pull this thing off. I bet you a nickel that you've thought many of the below thoughts:

- What will my supervisor and the people I supervise think of me?

- Will they see me as qualified?
- Will I be able to gain their support?
- As the new leader, am I supposed to know more about the project/program than the team already doing it?
- Can I meet the required time commitment levels?

See? I knew you've thought about these things. You owe me a nickel! Relax, your fears are valid, and every Power Leader has them.

CHALLENGES OF YOUR NEW ROLE

You are not a peer member anymore. You are no longer one of the guys (or gals). There are new expectations of you, and from those you now supervise, so be ready.

RESPONSIBLE FOR MORE THAN YOURSELF

It's no longer just about you. You now have to take on a parent-like role to ensure your workers' needs are met. For example, it's your responsibility to ensure all your workers (not just you) complete their daily time cards; it's your responsibility to resolve conflict between employees; it's your responsibility to advocate and promote their careers; and more. Success in this area requires application of leadership principles.

ACTIVELY AVOID FAVORITISM

Yesterday you were a peer and joking with the guys; but now you are their supervisor, and you will have to task them, discipline them, reward them, and grade their work. This new interaction is gonna cause friction if you don't change your behavior now.

Whom you share morning coffee with, who's cube you visit frequently, which employee you have lunch with, etc. can send a signal that you favor them over others. This can lead to office jealousy and unnecessary tension. If you do these activities, then ensure you do them (or offer) with all of your workers.

Reducing the frequency, quantity, and type of social interaction you once had with your peers will make it easier to have those difficult conversation with them that are sure to come.

GAIN TRUST OF YOUR SUBORDINATES AND YOUR BOSS

A key goal you should strive for is to build trust between you and your team members, so that your workers align efforts and perform as a team. To measure how well that trust is growing, check out Bruce Tuckman's *Forming, Storming, Norming, and Performing* model. It describes stages of team effectiveness. I won't restate his principles here. You can check it out on the Internet. When you understand it, you can help your new team become effective more quickly.

Here are a few techniques that build trust:

MANAGE BY WALKING AROUND

President Lincoln built trust among his troops through meaningful, frequent, and honest communications. He did this by getting away from his desk and going out into the field. He made himself available to his troops, one-on-one. They discussed the good, bad, and ugly of work performance, and the troops loved it! They didn't necessarily need Lincoln to solve their issues, but they did need him to listen to them. I'd like to think that Lincoln also benefitted from those conversations.

LEARN TRUTH IN THE BUSINESS UNIT

Like Lincoln did, inspect things yourself! As President, Ronald Reagan, used to say- "Trust but verify". Frequently there is a gap between how executive leaders 'think' things work, and how things 'really' work. The successful TV series "Undercover Boss" is based on this premise. In season one, episode one, the CEO of a large waste management company went undercover as a regular waste management worker. He discovered that a regional office manager was performing the work of four different people, and hadn't had a raise in a long time. The office manager battled cancer, had multiple families living with her, and never complained. The boss thought things were working well, but armed with this new firsthand knowledge (ground truth); the boss recognized the injustice as a significant deviation from standards, and placed her on salary, promoted her to supervisor, authorized her to hire her replacement, and become bonus eligible.

You should be like Ronald Reagan, Abraham Lincoln, and the CEO- regularly walk around and observe and ask questions. Does what you observe jive with policy, efficiency, and good business practice?

OFFER MEANINGFUL, FREQUENT, AND HONEST COMMUNICATIONS

A Power Leader who communicates meaningful information, openly and frequently, builds trust with team members. Can I convince you to host morning coordination meetings, or 5 minute morning stand-up meetings, or weekly progress meetings? Would you consider sending regular emails, email newsletters, or video messages to keep your staff informed.

Your demonstration of frequent and meaningful communication sets a tone that you value communication, and also has the added benefit of setting your operational tempo (battle rhythm), to keep productive momentum going. See more in Strategic Communications section.

UNDER-PROMISE AND OVER-DELIVER

Be mindful of over-promising results, when you might not be able to deliver them. While promising the moon may make you sound awesome now, failing to deliver the moon will cause people to doubt your word. I remember watching an episode of Star Trek Next Generation, where the original 1960's ship's engineer, 'Scotty', made a cameo appearance. He was mentoring Geordie LaForge (the current ship's engineer) that he should never tell the Captain how few hours it really takes to repair the ship's warp engine. Scotty goes on to explain that he wanted to be known as a "miracle worker" when he finished repairs sooner than expected. You too, might consider under promising results, so people will respect your capacity to deliver as promised.

WHO LEADERS & MANAGERS GO TO WHEN THEY NEED ADVICE

A Power Leader also seeks mentors from outside of the organization. Be sure to include government, NGO, Universities, and private industry as part of your professional support groups. Consider joining local business groups such as the Chamber of Commerce, Rotary Club, Foundations; and professional associations such as the International Association of Chiefs of Police, or the Society for Human Resource Management. Power Leaders across the globe share similar issues, and the different industry perspectives can reveal innovative solutions.

What the Boss Expects

Chapter 4

We all report to somebody. So how do we ensure that the Power Leader earns the respect, trust, and appreciation of his/her supervisor? The following are topics your boss wishes you knew, but he probably won't tell you...and you should expect of others *you* supervise.

Objectives When you complete Chapter 4, you will be able to: • Describe five activities your boss expects from you, but might not communicate it	**Terms** • TYLY

REGULAR COMMUNICATION

Regular communication with your boss on the status of activities and projects is a good way to earn respect, trust, and appreciation; especially when your supervisor doesn't have to ask for report updates. They just arrive. The reporting should contain monthly/weekly information that includes this year performance vs last year performance (TYLY) and ratio reporting, schedule status, spending status, performance status, variations from expectations, etc. Anticipate questions your supervisor might ask or would want to know. The Power Leader stays on top of regular reporting.

No surprises

Your role is to serve and support your boss. A good way to earn respect, trust, and appreciation is to keep your boss informed of things that could otherwise catch her off-guard. You want your boss to know of the good or bad news *before* they hear it from any other source. The last thing you want is your boss to be in a meeting and not know of something that you knew about, but didn't tell her. Don't let your boss be surprised.

Consider political Consequences

Your boss wants you to make good decisions, and that means you also consider the political consequences of your decisions, among other factors. Ask yourself how your decision will affect the reputation of your organization and your boss, in the eyes of other government departments, the pubic, and the media.

Deliver solutions to problems

Don't be a complainer. Instead, be a problem identifier, who also has one or more solutions to offer. Enough said.

Think Like an Executive

You may not be at the top of the executive food chain but that doesn't mean you can't think and act like you are. In other words, your boss shouldn't be the only person thinking ahead. If you have a business problem or new idea, then do the work to solve your way though it...even though no one asked you to. Forecast your overtime use, determine future manpower needs, conduct organizational assessments, create process maps, look for efficiencies in your business unit, and propose new ideas. Start acting like the role you want to fill. You get the point.

One method for communicating your ideas is to write a 'whitepaper'. See the chapter on Whitepapers for how to do this.

PART II

TOOLS & TECHNIQUES

Organizations without a clear vision switch from one task to another, wasting time and resources. The vision statement should provide the basis for everything the organization does.

Now stop reading and go look up other vision statements on the Internet. What's Amazon's vision statement? What kind of world does Amazon want to create?

Now You Try it!

Write a Vision Statement for your organization.

We are building a world where...

____

____

____

____

Mission Statement

So, now that you've described what kind of world your organization wants to create, let's talk about the activity that your organization and team will carry out to create that world. This activity becomes your *Mission*.

So why is a mission statement important? What does it do for you? It defines your business unit's role in accomplishing the vision (that future world). It defines what the organization does and doesn't do.

Without a mission statement, an organization may do stuff that doesn't lead to achieving its vision. Kind of like Starbucks making car transmissions instead of coffee. It just doesn't make sense.

Starbuck's mission statement is: *"To inspire and nurture the human spirit – one person, one cup and one neighborhood at a time."* (Starbucks 2017). They do stuff to nurture the human spirit, such as- sell pleasurable coffee and make heart designs in the latte foam; buy their coffee from responsible sources; construct their coffee cups from sustainable materials, etc.

The Los Angeles Police Department's mission statement is "*to safeguard the lives and property of the people we serve, to reduce the incidence and fear of crime, and to enhance public safety while working with the diverse communities to improve their quality of life"*. They do stuff to safeguard lives and property; they reduce crime; and they improve the quality of life. You can see these activities in action through the programs they deliver (patrol, investigations, community policing, volunteer, etc.)

Organizations without a clear mission cannot define their goals, they waste resources; and they can't establish strategies for success. The mission statement provides clarity for what the team or organization does and doesn't do.

This is an interesting mission statement...The Maryland Department of Transportation's mission statement reads: *The Maryland Department of Transportation is a customer-driven leader that delivers safe, sustainable, intelligent, and exceptional transportation solutions in order to connect our customers to life's opportunities.* This mission statement is a bit different in that it combines the vision, mission, and values statements into one statement, which is okay too. Here is their mission statement separated into the three statements?

> VISION: to connect (via transportation) customers to life's opportunities (where people live, work, play)
>
> MISSION: delivering exceptional transportation solutions
>
> VALUES: customer-driven, safe, sustainable, intelligent

Now stop reading and go look up other mission statements on the Internet. What are the vision and mission statements of the

Washington, D.C. Department of Human Resources? Examine them. Will their mission activities help achieve their vision? Are they aligned?

NOW YOU TRY IT!

Write a mission statement for your organization.

Our organization exists to ...

____

____

____

VALUES STATEMENT – A values statement (also known as corporate 'core values') is a fancy term used to guide decision-making and build corporate culture and promotes a reputation. It encourages behaviors and choices that an organization wants you to make. For example, if your organization values *speed*, then decisions and significant effort will be placed on behaviors and decisions that lead to urgency. If your organization values *safety*, then employees will choose the safer solution, as opposed to more effective but unsafe solutions. If your organization values *accuracy*, then decisions that improve correctness will be chosen.

Your corporate culture is will be built around its values, so choose them wisely watch your culture grow.

So why is a values statement important? What does it do for an organization? The values statement solves three challenges for the Power Leader.

1. Helps the Power Leader build a desired organizational culture, and

2. Helps workers make decisions, and
3. Defines what good or bad employee behavior looks like

A values statement is used to help workers make impactful decisions. When you are faced with multiple solution options to solve an issue, choose the one that best aligns with the value statements.

A values statement is also really useful for defining what good or bad employee behavior looks like. For example, when a Power Leader is faced with an employee who has a bad attitude, it's often hard to discipline that employee, because it's difficult to verbalize what "bad attitude" looks like. Frequently it can be difficult to tie poor behavior or performance to a specific agency policy.

But a good values statement defines what poor behavior looks like. A Power Leader then has substantial standing to discipline a problem employee- that is, for violating a corporate core value. For example, RESPECT: We respect and honor the dignity of each person, embrace civil discourse, and foster a diverse and inclusive community.

So, it's a good idea to include in your values statement the specific employee behaviors that a Power Leader wants and doesn't want.

For a real-world example of a values statement, Penn State University has a good one:

> INTEGRITY: We act with integrity and honesty in accordance with the highest academic, professional, and ethical standards.
>
> RESPECT: We respect and honor the dignity of each person, embrace civil discourse, and foster a diverse and inclusive community.
>
> RESPONSIBILITY: We act responsibly, and we are accountable for our decisions, actions, and their consequences.

DISCOVERY: We seek and create new knowledge and understanding, and foster creativity and innovation, for the benefit of our communities, society, and the environment.

EXCELLENCE: We strive for excellence in all our endeavors as individuals, an institution, and a leader in higher education.

COMMUNITY: We work together for the betterment of our University, the communities we serve, and the world."

A good statement contains text that describes how workers will demonstrate the core value.

Work cooperatively with your team to come up with vision, mission, and values statements. In this way, you will gain team buy-in and acceptance. Publish them and watch your healthy organizational culture start to form.

Remember to emphasize your vision, mission, and values statements with every new employee. Include them in your bonus/award programs; and assess adherence to them during annual employee performance reviews. More on this in the chapter on improving employee performance.

Organizations with a clear values statement that is encouraged and regularly communicated will build a healthy workplace culture.

Now, stop reading and go look up other values statements on the Internet. What's Northrup Grumman's values statement? Is there anything in there about how employees are to treat each other?

NOW YOU TRY IT!

Write a values statement, consisting of three values, for your organization. We will demonstrate < *value name here*> by <*the behavior here*>". Repeat this sentence for each of your values.

____

____

____

____

____

____

____

S.M.A.R.T. Goals

Chapter 6

Organizational goals optimize your resources and help you achieve your mission. Otherwise, your organization is like a leaf drifting in the wind; you wind up wherever the wind takes you. But, if you have well-formed goals, then you are like a ship with a rudder, you arrive at your intended destination.

Objectives	**Terms**
When you complete Chapter 6, you will be able to: • To write effective organizational goals, that are-specific, measurable, achievable, relevant, and time-bound administrative • To Describe the four sets of goals to manage	• Amount of Change • Direction of Change • Specific • Measurable • Achievable • Relevant • Time-Bound

There are goals that are clear and measurable, and then there are goals that are ambiguous and you're not really sure if you've achieved them. The more specific, measurable, achievable, relevant, and time-bound (S.M.A.R.T.) a goal is, the better. If your goals fit each of the S.M.A.R.T. elements, then you know you've got a good goal. Then you will have fewer arguments and misaligned expectations.

S.M.A.R.T. Goals

(S)PECIFIC

Means that a more detailed goal is better than a vague one. This means a good S.M.A.R.T. goal is clear and leaves little room for interpretation. It describes who, what, when, where, and how of your effort. For example, if your goal is about a geographical region, then be specific with the region. Define the boundaries of the region. Perhaps mention specific street names, or neighborhood names, or zip codes. If your goal is about finance, then be specific about which budget categories or line items. If your goal is about facilities, then which facilities specifically, which part of the facility? If your goals are about programs, then describe which part of the program, where it is based, its population that it serves, etc.

(M)EASURABLE

Means you define tangible metrics (things) that you will count to measure progress toward the goal. If your S.M.A.R.T. goal is specific enough there should be a unit to measure it by (attendees, meters, minutes, number of complaints, etc.). A measurable goal will usually answer questions such as- How much? How many? To what numerical level?

Specifically, a good measurable goal requires two elements-

1. A defined amount of change. For example, 23 items, 4 workers, eastern region, 5%, 25%, etc., and

2. A direction of change (increase or decrease). For example, *to increase by 15%*, or *to decrease by 30 occurrences*.

(A)CHIEVABLE

A good S.M.A.R.T. goal should have a realistic chance of being accomplished. While the goal may stretch a team's capabilities in order to achieve it, the goal is still realistically attainable, and not too extreme. That is, the goals are neither out of reach nor below expectations.

(R)ELEVANT

A good S.M.A.R.T. goal should be within your team's mission, and lead towards realizing the vision. If your goal meets these two criteria, then good. Otherwise, your goal may not be a good one and maybe it should be discarded. For example, a relevant goal for a Budget office, could be to deliver an official financial report within 30 days after the end of a fiscal year. Contrary, it's not relevant for the Budget office to make a goal to create two new baseball fields- it's just not relevant to their mission.

(T)IME-BOUND

A good goal has defined start and end dates. So, put due-by dates on your goals (and on every task you assign). Projects and goals can drag on indefinitely if you don't clearly indicate a due date. Due dates firm up shared expectations and help workers prioritize tasks.

CASE EXAMPLE

Assume you're a city administrator, and you want to make a S.M.A.R.T. goal for solving illegal parking problems in a business district. Which of the below two goals is more S.M.A.R.T.?

> *Goal A - "Reduce the number of illegally parked cars in the area of Town Hall"*
>
> *Goal B - By July 1, 2019, reduce the number of illegally parked cars by 25%, within a one mile radius of the Town Hall."*

Goal B is the better S.M.A.R.T. goal, right? It is specific and describes in measurable detail the geographic region affected. It's measurable by both geography and counting the number of illegally parked cars. A 25% reduction seems attainable to achieve. Reducing the number of illegally parked cars is certainly relevant to the mission of a police department or parking enforcement office. The goal is certainly time-bound to the exact days involved.

TWO QUICK POINTS ABOUT GOALS

For two reasons, some managers needlessly get stressed over developing goals:

First, they worry they won't be able to meet their goals. Nonsense I say! The cool thing about goal development is that you (working with other managers) get to determine how high the bar is set. So, working together, set your goal targets to a level that's actually achievable (the 'A' in SMART), therefore will have a high probability of succeeding.

Second, managers get stubborn and claim that their goals are not measurable. Again, nonsense I say! All goals are measurable. If you can't directly measure the amount of work throughput, then look to measure its *quality*. For example, instead of a goal to process 23 paperwork applications, consider a goal to have 98% of the applications processed within a defined time constraint, or with less than 1 error for every 10 applications.

MULTIPLE SETS OF GOALS

A Power Leader manages four different sets of goals,

- Your Personal goals, and
- Your employees' professional development goals, and
- Business unit goals, and
- Organizational goals

All of the goals should align and support the organizational goals. Remember, as a Power Leader you should be invested in developing yourself, your staff, your business unit, and your larger organization. That's four sets of organizational goals (and four strategic plans). The plans don't have to be equally thought out and organized.

PERSONAL GOALS

You're smart. You and your staff have personal career goals that you want to accomplish. Maybe it's to become Director of such and such, or to achieve an accreditation level, etc.. You may have a rough idea of what you want to accomplish in your career. These are good things, so let's incorporate them into your plans.

Write down two of your personal goals that you want to accomplish within the next two years.

____

____

____

____

A QUICK NOTE ABOUT RESUMES

Can I convince you to change your perspective on the use of a resume? You see, a resume serves as a roadmap to outline what your professional career experience needs to look like so you can take on your desired role (a proactive approach). When people fall into the trap of seeing their resume as a trail of where they've worked and what they've accomplished, they wonder why they can't reach their professional destination and achieve their desired career position.

So, do the research and find out what education, training, experience, knowledge, skills, abilities, associations, memberships, awards, accomplishments, etc. that your future role will require, and set goals to fill in those experiences and accomplishments that your resume says you're supposed to have.

WORKERS' GOALS

Your staff also have personal career goals that you all want to accomplish. What will you do to help your staff achieve their goals?

Write down one S.M.A.R.T. goal for how you will facilitate your workers' goals.

____

____

____

____

BUSINESS UNIT GOALS

In addition to the organization's goals, your business unit should have its own set of goals, and they should align with the larger organizational goals.

Write down two of your <u>business unit</u> goals that you want to accomplish within the next two years. Make sure they align with the larger organizational goals.

____

____

____

____

The Boss's expectations

Though not mentioned in the four sets of goals above, you should know that your boss likely has her goals and expectations of *you* and for *your* business unit. All of these goals should align and support each other; and all goals should move your organization closer to achieving its mission.

Write down two of your boss's goals and expectations of you.

___

___

___

___

Strategic Planning

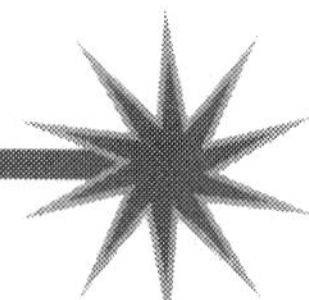

Chapter 7

Strategic Planning (mission planning) is the art of creating and attaching a custom strategy to each of your goals.

<table>
<tr>
<td>Objectives
When you complete Chapter 7, you will be able to:<ul><li>To develop an effective strategic plan that includes goals and strategies</li><li>To explain four dimensions to address in a strategic plan</li></ul></td>
<td>Terms<ul><li>Business Unit</li><li>Strategy</li><li>ROI</li></ul></td>
</tr>
</table>

Strategic Planning is arguably the single most important success ingredient for high-performing organizations, because it optimizes and aligns resources to provide the greatest return on investment (ROI). In other words, to get the biggest bang for the buck. Every separate business unit should have its own strategic plan to achieve its goals (not just one large plan for the entire organization).

EVERY SEPARATE BUSINESS UNIT SHOULD HAVE THEIR OWN STRATEGIC PLAN

The strategic plan *document* is the output of strategic planning work sessions; and becomes the guiding operations plan that directs work and aligns all organizational efforts.

Without a strategic plan, an organization lacks direction, wastes resources, lacks efficiency, suffers from low morale, and any success achieved are by definition, a fortunate accident.

STRATEGIC PLAN FORMAT AND CONTENT

Sample Strategic Plan Format

WELCOME STATEMENT
VISION/MISSION/VALUES STATEMENTS
DEVELOPING THE PLAN (AND DEFINITIONS)
OBJECTIVES (People, Process, Technology, Infrastructure)

People

Goal #1 Description
- Who responsible
- Strategy

Goal #2 Description
- Who responsible
- Strategy

Process

Goal #1 Description
- Who responsible
- Strategy

Technology

Goal #1 Description
- Who responsible
- Strategy

Physical Infrastructure

Goal #1 Description
- Who responsible
- Strategy

Figure 7.1 Strategic Plan Format

The Strategic Plan document can be structured/formatted any way you choose, and could address any set of mission dimensions of your organization. There could even be two versions, one public version that is more general; and an internal plan that is more detailed.

To get you started, a proven best practice for high-performing organizations is to organize the strategic plan around the four dimensions of People, Process, Technology, and Physical Infrastructure.

When we talk about the People dimension, we refer to hiring the right people, training them, compensation and rewards, and all things to enhance their performance.

When we talk about the Process dimension, we refer to how the workers do what they do. This includes policy, procedures, tactics, and techniques.

When we talk about the Technology dimension, we refer to software systems, paper forms (yes, paper is a technology), electronic files, communications, tools and equipment.

When we talk about Infrastructure dimension, we refer to buildings, chairs, office space, cubes, room temperature, geographic location, etc.

However, your organizational needs may be different, and it's okay to structure your plan around any dimensions you choose. As an example, one government organization structured their plan around the dimensions of Service, Technology, Efficiency, and Professionalism. They created a set of goals and accompanying strategies for each dimension.

Welcome Statement

This section introduces your strategic plan. You might consider writing the reasons for the goals you chose, or that you adhered to modern management best practices, and proclaim your agency's commitment to serving the public, etc. This a great place to boast and brag about your agency.

WELCOME STATEMENT

Dear Community Families, Businesses, and Employees,

Over the past three years, the <government> Office has kept its promise to keep families safe, businesses thriving, and employees prepared, through our crime prevention strategy. We have strengthened our partnerships with the community, reduced crime by 18%, improved our response to persons in mental health crisis, ...

Figure 7.2 – Sample Welcome Statement

Vision, Mission, and Values

This section offers the opportunity to showcase your agency and what it values.

MISSION STATEMENT

The <government> Office will strive to continuously improve safety and law enforcement services to all members of our community through improved Service, Technology, Efficiency, and Professionalism.

We will work interactively with federal, state, and other local law enforcement authorities to vigorously and fairly enforce criminal laws by ...

Figure 7.3 – Sample Mission Statement

Developing the Strategic Plan

This section describes how the strategic plan came about. What planning model you structured it by, etc.

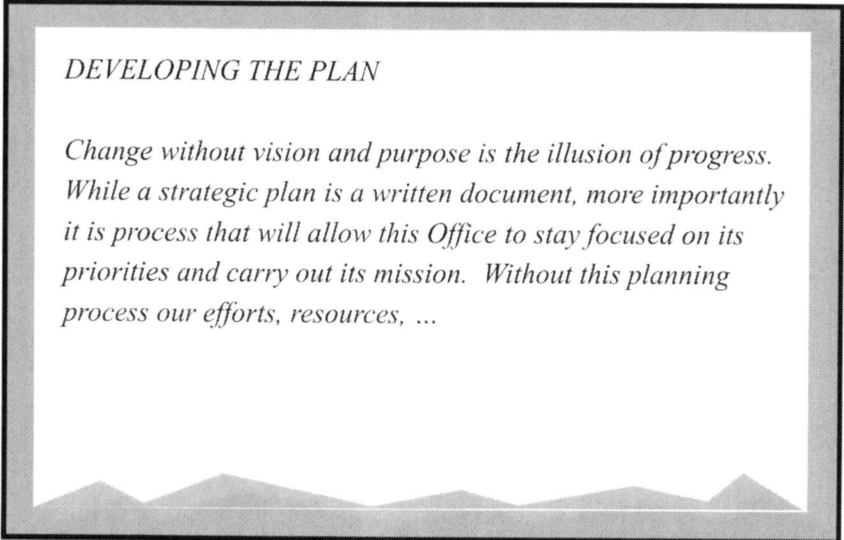

Figure 7.4 – Sample Developing Statement

Objectives

This is the 'meat' of the strategic plan. This section describes and the comprehensive coverage of issues with objectives and strategies! The objectives are made up of:

- Goals and metrics
- Person responsible
- Strategies

Under each dimension (People, Process, etc.), describe your objective with S.M.A.R.T. goals; define who is responsible for their success; explain your strategies, and define your metrics, etc. This book doesn't help you determine your strategies. That's up to you to figure out. Usually multiple strategies are applied at the same time in order to achieve your goal. For example, if your goal is to improve employee training, then you could employ both internal training capabilities and also expand external opportunities to train.

OBJECTIVES

SERVICE GOAL #1 *By June 30, 20xx, strengthen cyber crime investigative ability through research and development, ...*

Responsible Leadership Team: *Major XXX*

Strategy Description: *Assign a staff member as project manager to conduct research and create the recommendations document. Increase resources ...*

Figure 7.5 – Sample Objective

For each major business unit, consider having one goal under each of the four dimensions. For example, the Tax Assessment office could have one goal under People, and one goal under Process, and one goal under Technology, and one goal under Physical Infrastructure. A total of four goals.

Some organizations want a 20 year plan, others a 5 year plan, and others a one year plan. All of these time frames are good, with the one year plan being the most specific and measurable. Plans that are further out (5, 10, 20) are less specific and measurable, and give a general sense of what the organization wants to accomplish.

Now You Try It

Compose one goal & strategy in each for the four dimensions:

PEOPLE

GOAL # ______________

DESCRIPTION:

____

____

____

____

RESPONSIBILITY:

____

STRATEGY:

____

____

____

____

____

____

PROCESS

GOAL # ______________

DESCRIPTION:

____

____

____

____

RESPONSIBILITY:

____

STRATEGY:

____

____

____

____

____

____

TECHNOLOGY

GOAL # _______________

DESCRIPTION:

____

____

____

____

RESPONSIBILITY:

____

STRATEGY:

____

____

____

____

____

____

PHYSICAL INFRASTRUCTURE

GOAL # _______________

DESCRIPTION:

____

____

____

____

RESPONSIBILITY:

____

STRATEGY:

____

____

____

____

____

____

How to Identify Solutions

Chapter 8

A city manager could likely solve her challenges by any number of solutions, and each solution has its own costs in terms of money, time, political acceptance, lasting effectiveness, cost to maintain, level of effort to complete, etc. Choosing the optimal solution for your situation can be daunting. Here is a technique and a tool you can use to help you make better decisions.

Objectives When you complete Chapter 8, you will be able to: • Describe two techniques to select the optimal solution, from among competing solutions	**Terms** • Fix • Workaround • Optimize • Maximize

TECHNOLOGY VS BEHAVIOR SOLUTION

There are two broad categories that solutions fall into:

- Technology solution, or
- Behavior solution

As an administrator you can try one or both solutions, but do so with your eyes open, knowing that your solution doesn't always have to include adding or building something. Rather, know that your solution might be solved with just a behavior change.

To better understand the difference, consider traffic congestion as a city challenge to be solved. A *technology* solution could be to build more travel lanes or more roads. Yes, building roads and lanes is the application of technology; and more roads or more lanes would likely help ease congestion.

Now consider the costs of building these lanes and roads in terms of money, time, political acceptance, lasting effectiveness, cost to maintain, level of effort to complete. The costs could be significant.

As an alternative, and perhaps a first choice solution, consider a *behavior* change policy that could also resolve the traffic problem; such as to encourage carpools (maybe through a tax credit, HOV lane use, or other incentive).

Ask yourself, what are the costs in terms of money, time, political acceptance, lasting effectiveness, cost to maintain, and level of effort to complete? The costs and time to implement are likely less significant than the technology solution.

You see, the behavior solution could be implemented almost overnight, while the technology solution is generally more complicated. Both solutions might be equally effective.

To summarize, consider first trying behavior solutions, and if needed, supplement with technology solutions. What will your political and financial environment support?

Words to know:

What's the difference between a Workaround, and a Fix?

A Fix repairs and permanently resolves the problem. The issue goes away.

With a Workaround, the problem still exists, but the activity can still be successfully accomplished, but through other means that are more complicated or longer.

NOW YOU TRY IT

Think of a challenge that your organization faces. What are some possible technology solutions; and what are some possible behavior change solutions? Describe their costs in terms of money, time, political acceptance, lasting effectiveness, cost to maintain, level of effort to complete.

Behavior Solutions:

____

____

Costs

____

____

Technology Solutions:

____

____

Costs

____

____

DECISION MATRIX

Another way of choosing the optimal solution for your needs is through a Decision Matrix. A decision matrix is a weighted scoring tool that evaluates all of your solution options against multiple criteria (dimensions).

	FULLY RESOLVES ISSUE	IMPORTANCE WEIGHT	HIGH SCORE WINS
ADD ONE CARPOOL LANE	1	5	5
ADD ONE LANE	2		10
ADD TWO LANES	4		20
ADD TOLL LANE	3		15

	SHORT TIME TO IMPLEMENT	IMPORTANCE WEIGHT	HIGH SCORE WINS
ADD ONE CARPOOL LANE	3	2	6
ADD ONE LANE	3		6
ADD TWO LANES	2		4
ADD TOLL LANE	2		4

	LOW BUILD COST	IMPORTANCE WEIGHT	HIGH SCORE WINS
ADD ONE CARPOOL LANE	2	4	8
ADD ONE LANE	2		8
ADD TWO LANES	1		4
ADD TOLL LANE	4		16

	SUMMED RATINGS	FINAL SCORE
ADD ONE CARPOOL LANE	8 + 6 + 5	19
ADD ONE LANE	8 + 6 + 10	24
ADD TWO LANES	4 + 4 + 20	28
ADD TOLL LANE	**16 + 4 + 15**	**35**

Figure 8.1 Weighted Decision Matrix

In Figure 8.1, the solution options are:

- Add One Carpool Lane
- Add One Lane
- Add Two Lanes
- Add One Toll Lane

And the rating criteria are- 'Fully Resolves Issue', 'Short time to Implement', 'Low Build Cost'.

For each dimension, rate how well you determine the particular solution best meets the rating criteria. For example, the '*Fully Resolves Issue*' criteria, the 'Add Two Lanes' solution scored best - with a 4. For the '*Short Time to Implement*' criteria, the '*add one carpool lane*' and '*add one lane*' scored the best- with a 3.

Now assign a weight factor to each dimension. The weight factor represents how important each *dimension* is compared to each other dimension. In the example above, the most important criteria to meet is 'Fully Resolves Issue'- with a weight of 5.

Assign values for the rest of your criteria and weights to determine a cumulative score across all of your criteria.

Multiply the solution rating by the criteria weight value to calculate the index score (located in 'Highest Score wins' cell). For example, under 'Fully Resolves Issue' criteria, for the 'Add Two Lanes' solution, multiply 4 x 5 = 20. Also note that the 'Add One Carpool Lane' solution scored lowest for that criteria- 1 x 5 = 5.

For each solution, sum the index scores. For example, '*add one lane*' is 10 + 6 + 8 = 24. The highest cumulative score is your optimal solution. Have you figured out which is the optimal solution?

Here's how it works, step by step.

1. Decide on your available solutions
2. Decide on your criteria set
3. Under each criteria, assign a rating for how well each solution performs 1(poor) to 5(successful)
4. Assign a value to the 'Weight' of how important the criteria is to your decision-making 1(low) to 5 (high)
5. For each solution, multiply the solution *rating* value by the criteria *weight* value, to calculate the score
6. For each solution, sum the scores from all the criteria to get the final index score
7. The final index scores between solutions are compared. The highest index score wins.

A decision matrix results in an objective, data-driven model that reveals the optimal solution for your needs. For this example, 'add one toll lane' is the optimal choice with a score of 35.

You can also use this model for your public explanation of why you chose your winning solution. Something like "We objectively evaluated our options, and given the current cost, schedule, future maintenance costs, it's effectiveness, we selected the toll lane solution as our first measure to resolve the traffic congestion problem. Thank you for your support...blah...blah".

TIP! - You know, there's a difference between the words *optimize* and *maximize*. Maximize means the get the best return, even at extreme costs. Optimize means to get the best return for the cost expended.

NOW YOU TRY IT!

Pick three vacation spots, and use the matrix to help you decide which vacation to take:

____

____

____

____

____

____

OPTIONS	CRITERIA	IMPORTANCE WEIGHT	HIGH SCORE WINS

OPTIONS	CRITERIA	IMPORTANCE WEIGHT	HIGH SCORE WINS

OPTIONS	CRITERIA	IMPORTANCE WEIGHT	HIGH SCORE WINS

CRITERIA

OPTIONS	SUMMED RATINGS	FINAL SCORE

Which solution does your matrix recommend? Did it differ from what you thought the best solution was?

Author a Whitepaper

Chapter 9

So what's a 'whitepaper'? A whitepaper is not really white-paper. A whitepaper (one word) is a cool idea you have, that you write down and explain in a short 1-2 page document (electronic, paper, or otherwise), so you can convince others to implement your idea. It's a document.

Objectives When you complete Chapter 9, you will be able to: • Describe the purpose of a whitepaper, and list the five topics it should contain	**Terms** • Landscape • Challenge • Solutions • Risks • Next Steps

Give Life to Your Idea

You see, there's a difference between verbally telling someone your idea, versus communicating your idea in a document that can be shared and handed off to another for consideration. When you speak your idea, the words vaporize as soon as they are spoken; unlike a whitepaper that captures your idea and allows it to live on, most likely on someone's desk top. When you write a whitepaper, it gives life to your idea; your idea becomes a living thing that can't easily be forgotten or ignored. That's why your boss says "give me a write-up on that idea of yours". She's asking for a whitepaper.

The purpose of a whitepaper is to grab others' attention to your idea and persuade them to implement it.

THE PURPOSE OF A WHITEPAPER IS TO GRAB OTHERS' ATTENTION TO YOUR IDEA AND PERSUADE THEM TO IMPLEMENT IT

The reason it is short (1-2 pages) is to rise above time and attention grabbers. Think about it, you're more likely to read a 1-2 page document rather than a 25 page dissertation.

WHITEPAPER FORMAT

While the format of a whitepaper can vary, they are all meant to be short. You only want to pique the interest of the reader, not deliver a complete package. Once the initial eyebrow is raised that your idea is a compelling one, the next action would be a longer length feasibility study, or some more in-depth action.

Sample Whitepaper Format

LANDSCAPE/UNDERSTANDING

CHALLENGE/ISSUE/PLAN/PROBLEM IDENTIFIED

SOLUTIONS/RESPONSES/ACTIONS/OUTPUTS

RISKS/CONCERNS

NEXT STEPS

Figure 9.1 – Whitepaper Format

Since you have the short attention span of your reader, there are strongly recommended sections to get the most info across in the shortest amount of time. The title of the sections can vary depending upon the topic. Sometimes you're solving problems, other times, you're proposing an action.

Hear me now...your boss wants it short and to the point! No more than two pages. You should expect that of your workers too. When they come to you with an idea, ask them to submit a whitepaper to you. This will help them think through their idea, so later you both can speak intelligently about it.

LANDSCAPE/UNDERSTANDING

In this section you take one paragraph to describe the current state of your organization and introduce your idea.

Landscape
The Field Operations Division (Field Ops) wishes to gain insight into its operations and baseline its current workload. The following plan is a suggested roadmap for accomplishing this task. The outcome of this assessment is intended to:

- *Provide ground-truth, evidence-based information for the Division Commander to deploy resources efficiently and to meet service demands (deployment model)*
- *Determine baseline staffing for budget justification, and show variances over time to assist the Division Commander in determining strategic priorities*

Figure 9.2 – The Landscape

CHALLENGE/ISSUE/PLAN/PROBLEM IDENTIFIED

In this section you take several paragraphs to define the problem in some depth. Perhaps showcase some examples of the issue, add some statistics, and add some personal quotes.

Challenge
This workload analysis will be a 10 work-day level of effort- consisting of interviews, data research and analysis. The Assessor will validate with the Division Commander the business units to be evaluated:

- *Station 2,3,4,5 Crime analysis function*
- *Sample of patrol Sergeants*
- *Sample of Patrol Deputies*
- *Station 2,3,4,5 Civilian Support staff*

Figure 9.3 – The Challenge

SOLUTIONS/RESPONSES/ACTIONS/OUTPUTS

In this section you propose your suggested responses. Perhaps add statistics and graphics.

Output
The output for this project will be a low-level (detailed) report of the workload experienced by the Field Operations staff. It will also include a characterization of supporting workload elements that contribute towards job performance. The report will contain paragraph summaries, and supporting charts and graphs.

Figure 9.4 – Output

RISKS/CONCERNS

In this section you could include any risks or concerns and how you might mitigate each concern. If there are no issues or concerns, then you can comment that there are no concerns. Remember to describe the risk of doing nothing and maintaining the status quo.

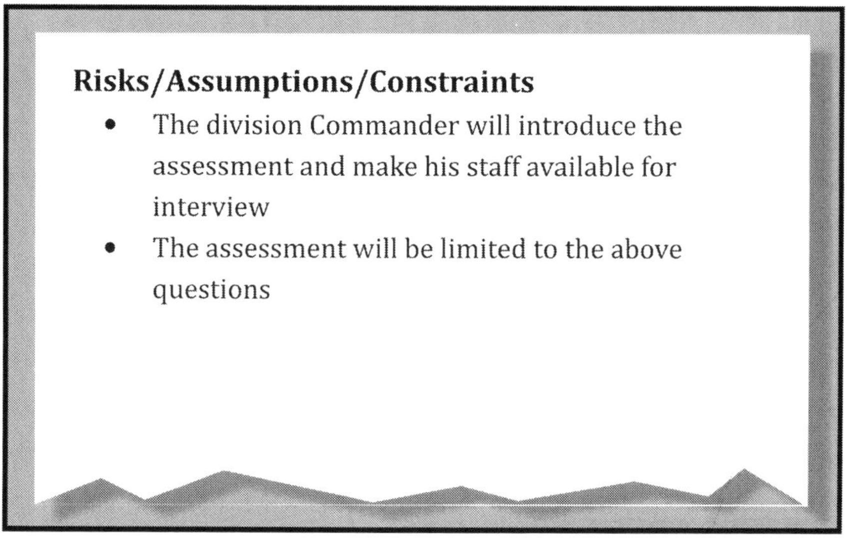

Risks/Assumptions/Constraints

- The division Commander will introduce the assessment and make his staff available for interview
- The assessment will be limited to the above questions

Figure 9.5 – Risks

NEXT STEPS

This section allows your idea to continue and not die. Don't make your boss come up with what actions to do next. You offer suggested next actions. Make it easy for her to say 'yes, implement your idea'.

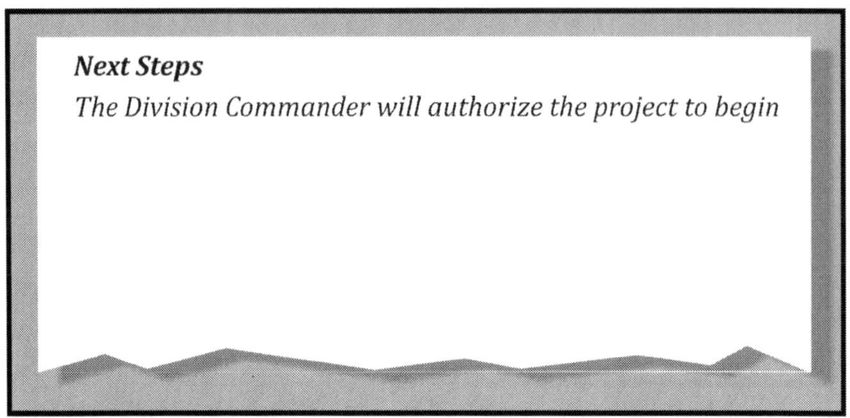

Figure 9.6 – Next Steps

A Word About Graphics

A super-huge part of your whitepaper is to give it a visual identity by branding it with a striking and informative graphic or logo. Often the reader of your whitepaper doesn't recall the title of the whitepaper, but they will recall that 'community model' logo you showcased, or that colorful chart that showed performance going up. Remember, this is about selling your idea and persuading others. In this case, sexy sells.

NOW YOU TRY IT

Think of an idea you've had. Under each section, write bullet points of what you might want to communicate.

WHITEPAPER TITLE
(logo goes here)

LANDSCAPE/UNDERSTANDING

____

____

CHALLENGE/ISSUE/PLAN/PROBLEM IDENTIFIED

____

____

SOLUTIONS/RESPONSES/ACTIONS/OUTPUTS

____

____

RISKS/CONCERNS

____

____

NEXT STEPS

____

____

Project Charter

Chapter 10

Whenever the boss asks you to do a project, the first step is to create a project charter document. It establishes a shared understanding of who is assigned the project, what roles/responsibilities/authorities that project team members have, high level schedule, constraints, success criteria, risks, and assumptions. The project charter is like a contract that you have with your boss.

Objectives When you complete Chapter 10, you will be able to: • Describe two techniques to select the optimal solution, from among competing solutions	**Terms** • Charter • Stakeholder • Scope • Deliverable • Constraint • Risk

Without a project charter, the exact goals and deliverables are not clear. There is no official management support. Risks aren't identified. Wrong assumptions are made. And the schedule and costs are undefined-defined. This is all bad and your program or project will likely fail.

The charter can be formal in a multi-page document, or can be as simple as an email. The important thing is to just have one.

Let me tell you a story that you could probably relate to:

Donna Director asks her subordinate, Sue Supervisor, to organize an employment recruiting event, and to deliver a high level plan for how she is going to manage it.

After leaving Donna's office, Sue sends an email out to her colleagues and other department stakeholders, asking them to join her for a kickoff meeting where they can discuss event requirements.

On the day of the kickoff meeting, only two of the eight colleagues show up. Sue is not really sure when the event plan is due back to Donna. She's not sure what Donna's expectations are. Sue is not sure of which stakeholders she should reach out to. The result is that Sue was not able to deliver the event plan document that Donna had envisioned.

Where did Sue go wrong? A project charter document would have been helpful here. A project charter is a written version of verbal reflection- "This is what I heard you ask of me. Do I have this right?"

With a Charter document, Sue would have the official authority to adjust others' work priorities and schedule people to attend the meeting; authority to acquire and spend the budget and other resources she needs; to understand what event timeline Donna had in mind; to understand the scope and outcome goals of the recruiting event, etc. And perhaps most important, the defined success criteria that would determine if the event was successful.

The following is an example of a project charter:

Project Charter

Promotional Assessment Project - March 21, 20xx

Project Description & Goal

The <government org> is transitioning from a contracted external promotional assessment process, to an internal ...

Project Team

The key project team is narrowed to:

- *Jim Smith – Project Manager*
- *Tim Brown – Subject Matter Expert*
- *Shannon Field - HR Coordinator Task Lead*

Key Stakeholders

- *Human Resources – Anna xxx, Brenda xxx (Impact)*
- *Legal – Susan xxx (Involvement)*
- *Strategic Planner – John Fernandes (Interest)*

Scope

The project scope contains the following elements:

- *Promotional Assessment is limited to assessing for Sergeant and 2nd Lieutenant positions*
- *The assessment outcome will be a pool of candidates, classified as Best Qualified, Qualified, and Unqualified.*

Deliverables

- *Job Dimensions list, with definitions*
- *Writing Exercise scenarios, Emergency Incident scenarios, ...*

Figure 10.1 – Project Charter

Budget
This project budget is capped at $8,000, to be used primarily for hotels, printing & binding materials. Previous budget for contracted assessment services was >$50K in 2016.

Schedule
Project start date will be January 2, 2017, with a completion date of April 30, 2017. The April completion date accommodates an opportunity for LCSO to implement its first assessment process on May 2.

Communications
The project manager will regularly communicate project status to the project sponsor in monthly reports.

Constraints
The project team is expected to apply only portions of their time to this project.

Risks
It's unknown when the new HR coordinator employee is not yet on board, and is not expected to contribute to the creation of the process; but is expected to coordinate beginning May 3.

Figure 10.1 – Project Charter (continued)

Now You Try It

Create a project charter for your project or program.

Project Charter

Project Name : ______________________________

Project Description & Goal

____

____

____

Project Team

____

____

Key Stakeholders

____

____

Scope

____

____

____

____

Deliverables

____

____

Budget

____

____

Schedule

____

____

Communications

____

____

____

Constraints

____

____

Risks

____

____

Program Management

Chapter 11

In an earlier chapter, you created the world's best strategic plan, now what do you do with it? How do you put it into action? Answer- you apply the learned management tools and, and hold regular (monthly or quarterly) program management reviews (PMRs) to monitor your progress towards achieving your goals.

Objectives When you complete Chapter 11, you will be able to: • To prepare a quad chart to communicate program status at a program management review	**Terms** • PMR • Quad Chart • Dashboard

THE PMR MEETING

What's a PMR? A PMR is a gathering of all the relevant executives, relevant program and project managers, and other key stakeholders for program managers to present and discuss the progress, successes, and problem areas for how well their strategic plan is working.

The PMR is meant to be a positive experience where managers can showcase their program. The goal of the PMR and the presentation document is to give executives a summary on the status and health of the program or project so they can acknowledge the good performance, and the opportunity to intervene and supply resources or guiding action to get back onto the strategic plan.

If regular PMRs aren't conducted, then achieving the strategic plan is in jeopardy. Goals and key milestones are missed. Poor strategies continue to fail. Senior executives don't have insight into their program health. A sense of 'who cares' begins to develop.

During the PMR, there will likely be discussions on program successes, rewards, issues and their root causes, and resolution strategies.

QUAD CHART FORMAT

PMRs presentations are generally delivered with a single page quad chart. A quad chart is a generic term for a presentation format that is a single page divided into four, five, or six sections (quadrants, or quads). Each section showcases a different component of the program that an executive would want to know about- schedule, scope, budget, milestones, completion status, staffing, successes/risks, etc.

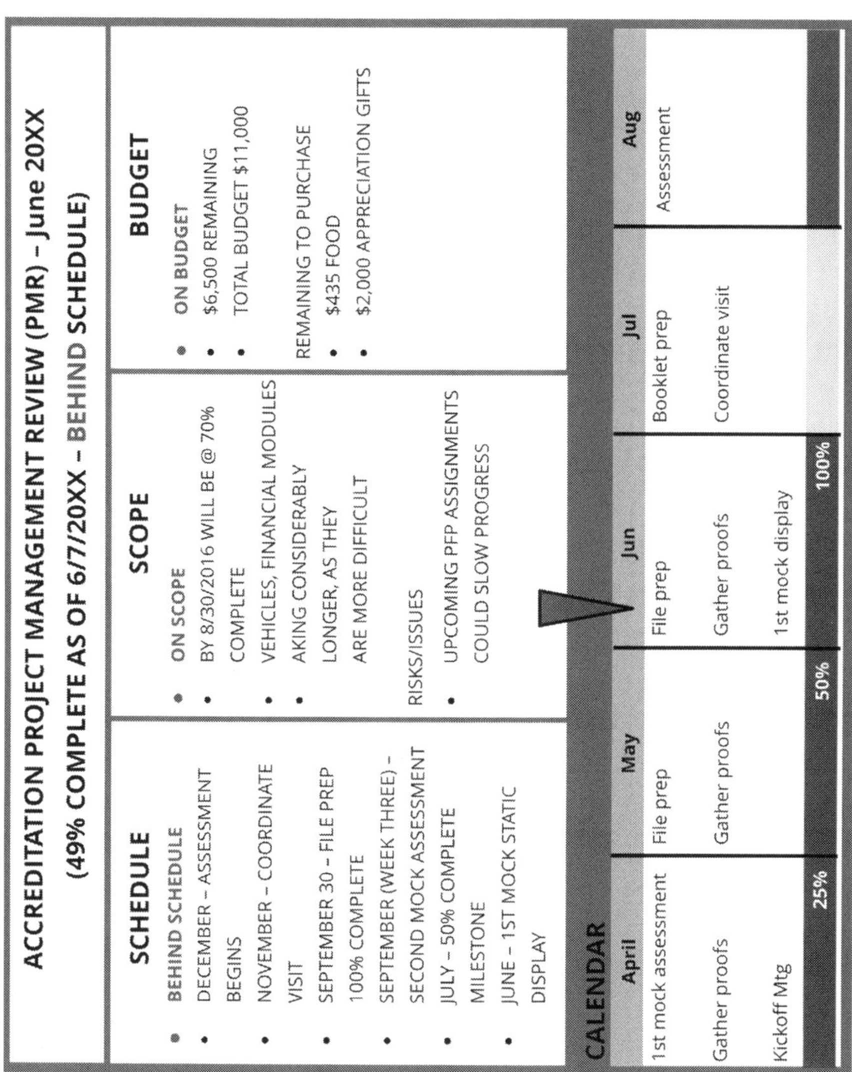

Figure 11.1 Sample PMR Quad chart

DASHBOARD FORMAT

You might have read about program or project 'dashboards'. A dashboard is an easy to read, highly visual display of the up-to-the-minute status of a program or project.

If you've ever watched a football game, then you've seen a dashboard. It's the banner at the bottom of the screen that shows the score, the quarter, how much time is remaining, and what down the play is on. It's up to the minute, easy to read, and highly visual. Public administrators regularly use dashboards too. Public safety uses them for emergency management status of roads, bridges, where vehicles are, etc. Fleet maintenance authorities use them for which government vehicles are in/out of service. Transportation authorities use them for road and traffic conditions.

While a quad chart is a type of dashboard, a quad chart is meant to deliver longer-term status. When people say 'dashboard' they mean the up-to-the-minute type.

POST PMR

When the PMR meeting is over, there should be next steps to reward good performance, fix things, implement new strategies, or recalibrate goals.

To track what was discussed and what the next steps are, consider the following sample post-PMR report to capture the discussed observations and recommendations. Be sure to maintain all historical versions and keep them in your project/program documentation.

POST PMR ACTION PLAN - AUG 20XX			
#	OWNER	Observation	Recommendation
1	JOE	PARKS AND REC DEPARTMENT COMPLETED THEIR SUMMER SPORTS RECREATION PROGRAM, WITH CITIZEN SATISFACTION RATE OF 99%.	REWARD MANAGEMENT STAFF WITH BONUS.
2	SUE	FIRE DEPARTMENT IS FALLING SHORT OF THEIR 3RD QUARTER RECRUITMENT GOALS. CAUSE IDENTIFIED AS INABILITY TO HIRE BEFORE 30 ...	AUTHORIZE A TEMPORARY EARLY HIRING POLICY, AND ASSIGN NEW EMPLOYEES TO SUPPORT TRAINING ...

Figure 11.2 – Post PMR Action Plan

NOW YOU TRY IT

Craft a one slide PMR quad chart of your program status:

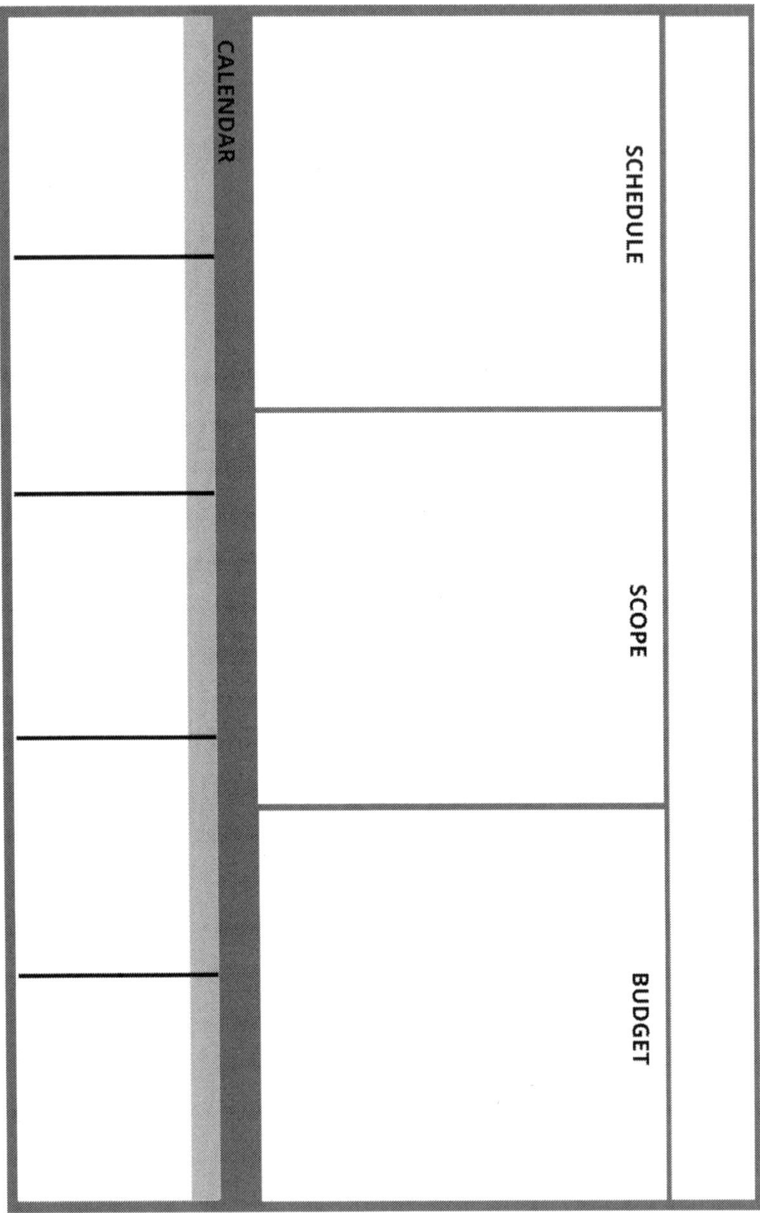

Phase Planning

Chapter 12

As you begin a new project, it helps to organize your thoughts on the project inputs, outputs, and what activities need to be done (and when), by using an *approach structure* broken down into phases. This structure displays bird's eye view of your project in one glance, and will help you and others understand what your project team will do, and how you will do it. The output of this approach planning session is an approach graphic (figure 13).

Objectives	**Terms**
When you complete Chapter 12, you will be able to: • Break down a large project into more understandable and achievable phases; to aid in planning	• Phase • Project vs Program • Approach • Baseline

Government programs always have one or more projects going on. Examples of projects could be a software systems upgrade, budget development 'season', opening a new facility, or developing a new public service (a Project transforms into a Program once it is placed into operation).

For this reason, let's spend time on project management best practices. For this case study, let's assume the boss has asked you to develop and execute a promotional assessment event, to take place three months from now. We'll use many of the tools and techniques presented earlier.

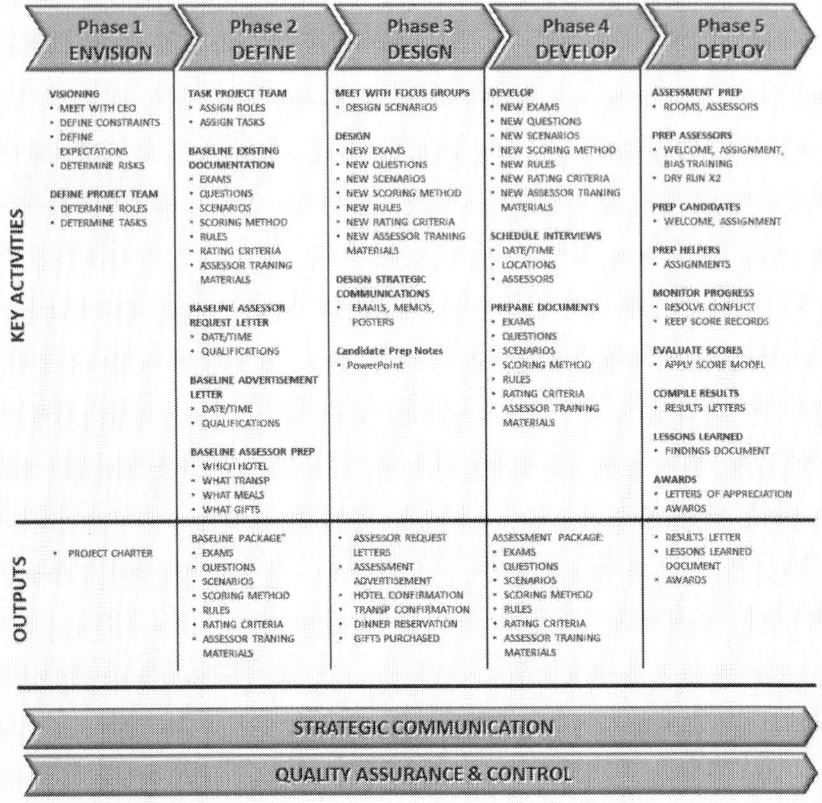

Figure 12.1 Approach Graphic

This graphic becomes your high level master plan that you can share with others. It is a management tool that helps craft the more detailed work breakdown structure and a Gantt chart to follow.

Notice in Figure 12.1, the inputs, tasks, and outputs during each phase of work. Notice that underlying all phases of work are regular strategic communications activities and quality assurance & control activities.

If you don't begin your project planning with such a high-level structure, then the upcoming WBS and Gantt charts will be disorganized, missing key tasks, and much more difficult to develop.

The approach graphic gives your brain a jump start to conceptualize the project as a whole.

APPROACH PHASES

The approach graphic is comprised of five time phases- Envision, Define, Design, Develop, Deploy. In each phase there are inputs, activities, and outputs. The outputs of one phase become the inputs to the next phase.

ENVISION PHASE

This phase is where you hold a kickoff meeting to gather and record what your CEO or Department Director has in mind for your project or program (the project Scope). Gather and document her vision, expectations, expected due dates, authorized budget, which workers are permitted to work on the project team, success criteria, and constraints.

After this kickoff meeting, do some research to be able to provide a rough estimate of what resources and time you will need to successfully complete the project, given the vision that your CEO has in mind. Create a high-level approach graphic to help you get a rough estimate of the scope, cost, schedule, and resources you will need.

Return to your CEO with your approach graphic, cost, schedule, and resource estimates and negotiate to nail down the final approved amounts. Combine these values with the previously discussed constraints, risks, success criteria, etc. and this document becomes your Project Charter document and serves as your official marching orders from upper management. 10% of your total project effort is spent here.

The output of the Envision phase is a Project Charter document.

WARNING! Until you receive the CEOs signature on the Charter (her approval), you shouldn't waste your time and effort on the project. It will be doomed to failure from lack of executive level support.

DEFINE PHASE

In this phase, you've received approval from your CEO to begin, and you start to research the current state of your project, and take inventory (baseline) of what tools, materials, documents, people, process, technology, and infrastructure, etc. that you have to work with.

By analogy, if your airplane crash-landed on a deserted island, you take inventory of what food, water, clothing, shelter, medical supplies, and communication survived the crash. This stuff becomes your baseline of what materials you have to work with.

For your project or program, conduct an inventory baseline to find out what documentation already exists. What work was already started/completed on the project before you arrived? What the experience of the team who did this project last year. What worked and what did not. What performance metrics were captured in the past? Where was the work completed? What facilities were used? What software is available? What transportation is available? Who are your stakeholders and what level of reporting do they require. 10% of your project effort is spent here.

The output of this phase is a solid understanding of the as-is condition of your project- what materials, people, processes you have to work with moving forward.

DESIGN PHASE

In this phase, you determine what final output products you want (documents, training materials, policies) and what things you want to be sure are included in them.

Considering the promotional assessment as an example, consider what information you want in the PowerPoint training materials; consider what information you want in the policy documents, consider what information you want in the scenarios, decide to conduct focus groups to develop the scenarios and interview questions.

is this phase you combine the findings from the Envision phase (project Charter, along with scope, cost, schedule, resource estimates), and the findings from the Define phase (baseline inventory), and use them to outline the tasks and schedule for how you will go about creating the master plan (your approach). A Gantt chart (a WBS with time added to it) is the usual output of this design phase. It is a calendar-based schedule of all tasks and how long they will take to complete. It outlines what comes first, second, which tasks can occur at the same time, etc.

You could split this Design phase into two parts, first the high-level discussion part is where you discuss with your project planning team all the work packages of the project that need to be created. Considering the promotional assessment as an example, you define how many questions will be on the exam; how many scenarios you want to create; do the number of questions and scenarios fit within your timeline? How many assessors will you need? Which hotel will they stay in? What transportation will you select? What training materials will you need? Perhaps you discover that you will need to create rating criteria, and update a rules/policy document.

The second part, of Design phase is where you discuss with your project planning team the order you want to create the above work packages, how long each work package will take, what resources each work package will need, who will be responsible for each work package, etc. This is where you create your Gantt chart. Considering the promotional assessment as an example, you might find that creating scenarios and creating assessor training materials can be created at the same time and each will take approximately one week each; while reserving assessor hotel rooms will take one day but must come after defining which assessors will participate.

At this point, you're still in the planning phases. You're not developing/building anything yet. 40% of your effort is spent here.

A WBS and a Gantt chart are the usual outputs of this design phase.

Develop Phase

In this phase you take in the WBS and Gantt chart from your design phase and actually build what you designed. Considering the promotional assessment as an example, you build the PowerPoint training materials, you author the policy documents, you create the scenarios, you conduct focus groups, you validate findings, etc.

A lot of your management expertise is spent here coordinating activities, ensuring their product quality is good, and reporting on the project progress. 30% of your effort is spent here.

The outputs of this phase are the actual completed products and materials your project is meant to accomplish.

Deploy Phase

In this phase you take the products you created and put them into service. If this were a new software package, you install the software on everyone's computer.

Considering the promotional assessment as an example, you transport the assessors and welcome them. You train and prep them for the day's activities. You collect the assessor ratings.

Your management expertise is spent here coordinating activities; ensuring things go smoothly and manage project progress.

After the project event has been deployed, it now becomes the responsibility of a program manager. The difference between a project and a program is that a project has definite start and end dates. It's temporary. On the other hand, a program is a continual effort with now end. Frequently, projects evolve into ongoing programs. The project part was to get the program started and into production. 20% of your effort is spent here.

As you can see, Phase planning helps you understand your project from a time and task perspective, and the resulting graphic helps you communicate your plan.

The Approach Graphic showcases of a number of smaller supporting projects and roughly when they will be accomplished. Review the inputs, tasks, and outputs during each phase of work. Notice that underlying all phases of work are regular strategic communications activities and quality assurance & control.

SUMMARY

The approach graphic showcases the project activities and communicates roughly in what time order they will be accomplished.

As you can see, Phase planning helps you understand your project from a time and task perspective, and the resulting graphic helps you communicate your plan.

Terms to grow by:

There's a difference between a Program and a Project. A Program is a continuous and ongoing endeavor, with no end. While, a Project is a temporary event having a definite start and a definite end date.

NOW YOU TRY IT

Craft a high level phase plan graphic for your project that demonstrates all five phases, inputs, outputs.

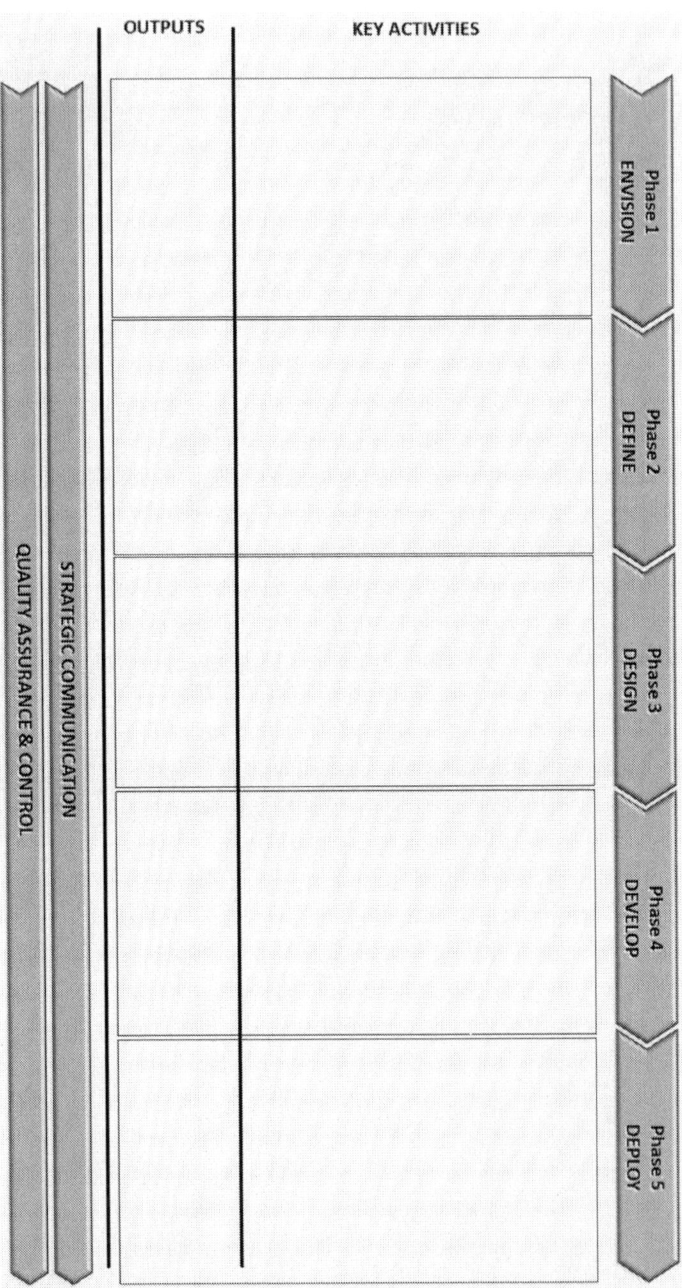

Estimate Resources

Chapter 13

How do you eat an elephant? Well, one bite at a time of course! Likewise, when you plan a large project it's difficult to identify and estimate resources looking at your project as one big animal. The better approach is to break the project down and deconstruct it into smaller, more manageable activities, resulting in a *work breakdown structure*.

Objectives	**Terms**
When you complete Chapter 13, you will be able to: • To accurately estimate the time and resources needed to complete your project	• WBS • Work Package • Man-hours

Without a work breakdown structure (WBS), you will likely mis-calculate how much time, money, and resources it will take to complete your project; you might miss important sub-tasks; and you might find it more confusing to manage the whole project.

3X5 Work Breakdown Structure

Regardless if you're project is to build an aircraft carrier or make a peanut butter and jelly sandwich, break down (deconstruct) your

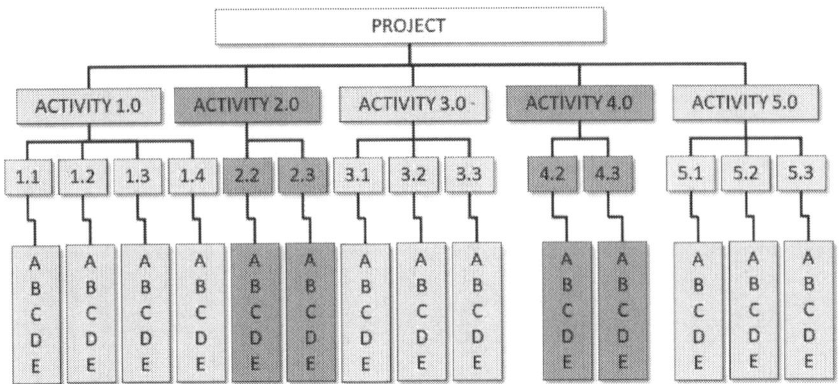

project into no more than three (3) tiers of no more than five (5) activities (work packages) at each tier.

Figure 13.1 – 3x5 Work Breakdown Structure

- (Tier 1) Deconstructs the project into no more than 5 work packages
- (Tier 2) Deconstructs each of the top tier work packages into no more than 5 sub work packages
- (Tier 3) Deconstructs each of the tier 2 work packages into 5 more sub work packages of its own

When complete, you might have a total of three tiers, and up to five activities, for a possible total of 125 work packages. Note: You may not need five activities at each tier, or all three tiers.

Notice that a WBS only lists tasks, it does not take into consideration the sequencial order in which they will be accomplished (this comes later in a Gantt chart).

Working with smaller project parts (a.k.a. work packages) will help you better quantify, estimate, and manage all sorts of concerns, such as- identify all the involved tasks, estimating task duration, estimating costs, estimating schedule, estimating staffing, identifying equipment, conference room space, and other resources.

HOW TO BUILD A WBS

Create increasingly detailed products that describe the tasks, time, and resources. Each product is for a different purpose (briefings or operations) and contains just the right amount of project detail for that purpose.

Start with the project approach structure (previous chapter) and notice that it contains high-level information. Expand each of its key tasks into more detailed 3x5 information; something like the following WBS figure:

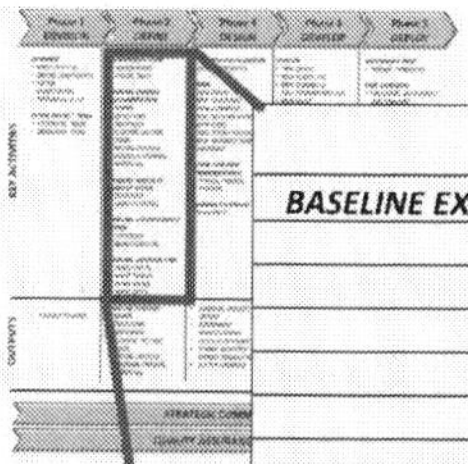

DEFINE			
BASELINE EXISTING DOCUMENTATION	TASK LEAD	**COSTS**	**MAN-HOURS**
	EXAMS		
	QUESTIONS		
	SCENARIOS		
	SCORING METHD		
	RULES		
	RATINGCRITERIA		
	ASSESSOR TRANING MATERIALS		
	TOTAL		
ASSESSOR REQUEST LETTER	TASK LEAD		
	DATE/TIME		
	QUALIFICATIONS		
	TOTAL		
ADVERTISEMENT LETTER	TASK LEAD		
	DATE/TIME		
	QUALIFICATIONS		
	TOTAL		
ASSESSOR PREP	TASK LEAD		
	HOTEL		
	TRANSP		
	MEALS		
	GIFTS		
	TOTAL		

Figure 13.2 – WBS

ASSIGN ESTIMATED HOURS, COSTS, AND STAFF

Here's the magic of a WBS. Now that a complete listing of all the tiered tasks have been identified, estimate how many hours, how much budget, and how many staff and other resources each task (work package) will take:

- Man-Hours – how many man hours do you estimate it will take to fully complete this particular task? Man-hours is defined as the total number of working hours applied to task completion, regardless if applied by one person or more than one person. (Ex. 2 people @ 4 hours each = 8 man-hours).
- Costs – what financial costs will this particular task consume?
- Staff – which staff member is the sole person responsible to ensure the particular task is completed. This person is known as the 'Task Lead'. How many staff will she need?

EXAMPLE WBS

Let's create a WBS for an agency's promotional process.

The promotional process was decomposed into five tier 1 activities- Envision, Define, Design Develop, Deploy. (Does this look familiar?)

DEFINE			
BASELINE EXISTING DOCUMENTATION	TASK LEAD - JOHN	**COSTS**	**MAN-HOURS**
	EXAMS	$0	3
	QUESTIONS	$0	3
	SCENARIOS	$0	3
	SCORING METHD	$0	3
	RULES	$0	2
	RATINGCRITERIA	$0	3
	ASSESSOR TRANING MATERIALS	$0	3
	TOTAL	**$0**	**20**
ASSESSOR REQUEST LETTER	TASK LEAD - MARY	$0	2
	DATE/TIME	$0	0
	QUALIFICATIONS	$0	0
	TOTAL	**$0**	**2**
ADVERTISEMENT LETTER	TASK LEAD - MARY	$0	2
	DATE/TIME	$0	0
	QUALIFICATIONS	$0	0
	TOTAL	**$0**	**2**
ASSESSOR PREP	TASK LEAD - JILL		
	HOTEL	$1,298	1
	TRANSP	$0	1
	MEALS	$642	1
	GIFTS	$392	4
	TOTAL	**$2,332**	**7**
		$2,332	**31**

Figure 13.3 - Assigned Man-Hours and Costs to WBS Tasks

Each of those tier 1 activities was further decomposed into up to five tier 2 activities. For example, in Figure 13.3, the Define phase, Assessor Prep task was decomposed into:

- Baseline Existing Documentation sub-task
- Assessor Request Letter sub-task
- Advertisement Letter sub-task
- Assessor Prep sub-task

And for each of the tier 2 activities, it is decomposed into no more than five tier 3 activities. For example, Figure 11, the Assessor Prep activity contains:

- Hotel
- Transportation
- Meals
- Gifts

Given the assigned man-hours, you realize the Define phase will cost $2,332 in materials and services (not including employee wages), and consume 31 man-hours.

Let's take a closer look at the WBS and see what more information we can determine:

- How many people will you need?
- Which tasks can be accomplished concurrently (at the same time)?
- Which tasks, if any, must be completed before another task can start?
- What is the shortest amount of time it will take to fully complete the Define activity?
- What is the longest amount of time it will take to fully complete the Define activity?

So you see, by creating a WBS, you end up with a fairly accurate estimate of the number of tasks, people, and hours it will take to complete your project. You use this information to help create your overall project calendar.

Author Note: In the example above, I know the Baseline Existing Documentation task contains 7 tasks instead of the suggested 5. But for this project, there were sooooooo many different types of related documents that we had to baseline- I kept it as is.

Now You Try It

Refer to your projcet plan approach you created in chapter 12 and craft a simple WBS (don't add costs, resources, or man-hours yet):

ACTIVITY-			
TASK:	TASK LEAD	COSTS	MAN-HOURS
	SUB-TASK		
TASK:	TASK LEAD		
	SUB-TASK		
TASK:	TASK LEAD		
	SUB-TASK		
TASK:	TASK LEAD		
	SUB-TASK		
	TOTAL		

Now, go back and assign estimated costs and man-hours.

RESULTS

- How many people will you need?
- Which tasks can be accomplished concurrently (at the same time)?
- Which tasks, if any, must be completed before another task can start?
- What is the shortest amount of time it will take to fully complete the Define activity?
- What is the longest amount of time it will take to fully complete the Define activity?

Did your cost and schedule findings differ from what you thought?

Task Sequence and Schedule

Chapter 14

From a previous chapter, I presented how to identify all the tasks in a project. In this chapter I present how to sequence them in your schedule, so you maximize your time, and reduce waste. We'll do this with a Gantt chart. A Gantt chart is a close cousin to a WBS (actually, it is a WBS on a calendar). Both tools list project tasks, but unlike a WBS, a Gantt chart actually sequences the tasks (which order they should go in). It will also show *dependencies*- what tasks have to begin before another, or complete before another begins, etc. It delivers a highly detailed list of all tasks sequenced over time.

Objectives	**Terms**
When you complete Chapter 14, you will be able to: • To prepare a Gantt chart to manage a project and communicate its status	• Gantt Chart • ROM • Parametric Estimation

A Gantt chart displays the earliest time a task can start, the duration of each task, the latest each task can complete, which tasks can occur at the same time, and project completion status. When you think 'Gantt', think 'schedule'. Project and Program managers work off of this chart, and update it daily.

If you don't create a Gantt chart, it is difficult to look at your project from a timing aspect and get a comprehensive view of what activities comes first, what activities come second, how long your project will take to complete, etc. Your order of activities could occur at the wrong times. Your resources might not be available when you need them. Cost overruns can occur; resources might not be available when you need them, etc.

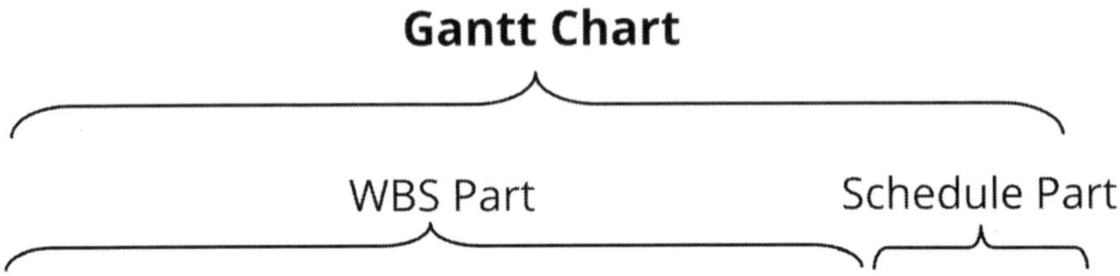

Gantt Chart

WBS Part — Schedule Part

ID	Task Group	Task	Task Lead	WEEK1	WEEK2	WEE
1	VISIONING					
2		MEET WITH CEO	JOHN			
3		DEFINE CONSTRAINTS	JOHN			
4		DEFINE EXPECTATIONS	JOHN			
5		DETERMINE RISKS	JOHN			
6	DEFINE PROJECT TEAM					
7		DETERMINE ROLES	JOHN			
8		DETERMINE TASKS	JOHN			
9	BASELINE EXISTING DOCUMENTATION					
10		EXAMS	CHRIS			
11		QUESTIONS	CHRIS			
12		SCENARIOS	CHRIS			
13		SCORING METHD	LINDA			
14		RULES	LINDA			
15		RATINGCRITERIA	LINDA			
16		ASSESSOR TRANING MATERIALS	LINDA			
17	ASSESSOR REQUEST LETTER					
18		DATE/TIME	Mary			
19		QUALIFICATIONS	Mary			
20	ADVERTISEMENT LETTER					
21		DATE/TIME	Mary			
22		QUALIFICATIONS	Mary			
23	ASSESSOR PREP					
24		HOTEL	BONNIE			

Figure 14.1 - Gantt Chart

Notice in Figure 14, that the tasks under 'Baseline Existing Documentation', can't start until the 'Define Project Team'. And the project team cannot be defined until the *visioning* activities are completed. To summarize, the Gantt chart coordinates activities and the time they can occur.

The Gantt chart can also show if your project is behind schedule, on schedule, or ahead of schedule. Look at the start and end times of each task. For example, if it's now week 3 of the project and the visioning tasks are not yet complete, then you are behind schedule. Likewise, the Gantt chart can show the percent of the project completed- by dividing the completed tasks by the total number of tasks to accomplish.

LET'S REVIEW

An *Approach Graphic* delivers a high level view of activities and timeline. Used for executive management to understand the project as a whole, without specific details.

A *WBS* is a detailed catalog of all required tasks, organized in a tree-like structure. No reference to time sequencing or dependencies.

A *Gantt chart* delivers a highly detailed list of all tasks (WBS) sequenced over time. How long each will take, and which tasks can occur at the same time, and project status. Project and Program managers work off of this chart, and update it daily.

Words to grow by:

Parametric Estimating. Hours per square foot, cost per square foot, cost per person, etc.

NOW YOU TRY IT

Craft a simple Gantt chart for your project:

ID	Task Group	Task	Task Lead	WEEK1	WEEK2	WEEK3	WEEK4	WEEK5	WEEK 6	WEEK7	WEEK8
1											
2											
3											
4											
5											
6											
7											
8											
9											
10											
11											
12											
13											
14											
15											
16											
17											
18											
19											

Process Improvement

Chapter 15

Business Process Improvement (BPI), also known as Business Process Reengineering (BPR), is a management skill used to highlight opportunities for business operations to function more efficiently. It uses *process maps* to understand how a particular business activity works- from beginning to end, to reveal opportunities to improve; or to help troubleshoot underperforming areas.

Objectives When you complete Chapter 15, you will be able to: • Use process maps to highlight areas for efficiency improvement	**Terms** • Process Map • Swim Lane • SME • Concurrency • Batching

THE PROCESS MAP

Creating a process map entails interviewing people and researching documentation so you can translate all the steps involved in a process, and put them on paper.

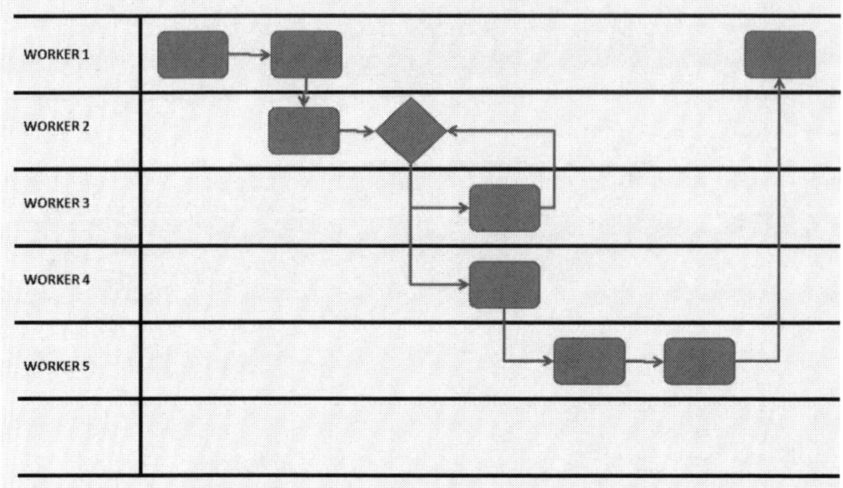

Figure 15.1 - Process Map

The output of *process mapping* activity is, wait for it....a *process map* (duh!). Sometimes a process map is called a *flow chart.* Once complete, the process map can be used to analyze how a business function can be made easier, more efficient, less costly, faster, or more effective.

If you don't make and use process maps, then you might miss opportunities for efficiency; or might not see the root cause of a business problem; or you might think a process happens one way, but in reality it doesn't. No matter how you look at it, you might be missing something important.

PROCESS MAP USES

A process map will answer questions such as-

- who are the people involved in the process;
- what process steps occur first, second;
- what paperwork is needed;
- what decisions are made;
- what are the inputs and outputs;

- and more...

In addition to seeking efficiencies, process maps can also be used to troubleshoot a business failure, or to facilitate process understanding.

For example, suppose your staff regularly consume overtime, or frequently submit their deliverables late. Why is that? If the employee can't easily answer the question, then work together to create a process map of each step in the process. If you observe an odd step in the process map that you didn't expect, then give a fist-pump because you've just found a gold nugget! You identified a disconnect between how you think things work versus how things actually work.

Process maps are a key input for root cause analysis. See also root cause analysis chapter.

PROCESS MAP FORMAT

A process map is formatted into a bunch of horizontal lines called swim lanes. It looks like swimming pool, right? Each swim lane represents a specific person (or group) who acts upon steps in the process (see figure 15.1).

In each of the swim lanes there are steps in the process (represented by blue boxes), that the worker performs. These boxes represent specific steps to act upon and include actions (verbs) such as 'estimate costs', 'check budget', 'approve', 'deny', 'review', 'record', 'gather data', etc.

The shape of the icons visually tell us something about what occurs in that step- a rectangle represents an action step, and a diamond represent a decision step (see figure 15.2). In the blue boxes, describe what action occurs in that step.

There are also arrows in the process that represent the next ordered step in the process. They connect steps within the swim lane, and they cross between swim lanes. There can sometimes be two processes that occur at the same time.

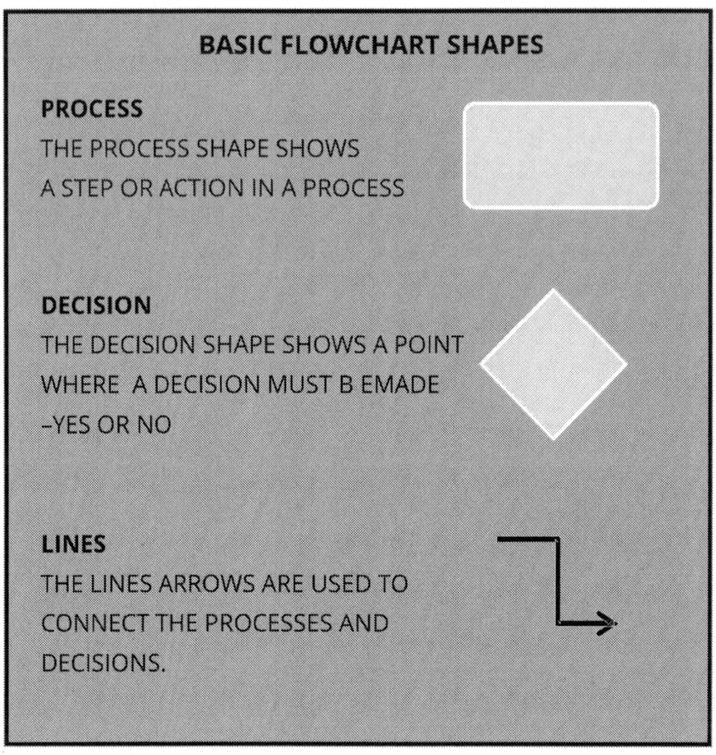

Figure 15.2 - Flowchart Shapes

The Mapping Interview

The process map begins with an interview of the subject matter expert (SME) of the business process you want to understand. An SME is someone who is sufficiently familiar with the process you want to examine.

For our example, let's say you want to understand how an employee requests and seeks approval for a training class to attend. First, you interview the training coordinator SME who actually does the work.

Methodically, have the SME list each step in the process. Interrupt him/her frequently. Ask questions about why that specific person must do that particular process. Could this be done by a less skilled worker? Instead of passing the product on to another, could they do the job at this step if they were given the authority to take action? Could this process occur at another time? How many hours/days does the process take?

Ask lots of *why* questions at each step. Even ask follow-up *why* questions of the previous *why* answer.

During the interview take notes and draw the described process on a whiteboard or notepad; and later copy the hand drawn map to PowerPoint or Visio to create your finished product.

PROCESS MAP ANALYSIS

Now that the map is completed. Review each step in the process and refer to your notes often. Examine the value that each step produces. Ask yourself if the step is really needed to produce the product to your quality standard. Eliminate it if not needed.

Sample questions to ask:

- Why is this step necessary?
- Can this decision be made by another person? (to avoid crossing swim lanes)
- Can the Power Leader give the person the authority to make the decision, and eliminate the step?
- Can this step occur earlier or later in the process?

Scrutinize the map and look for ways to shorten the process map, in both the vertical and horizontal directions.

1. Vertically (number of people involved). Look for ways to avoid crossing swim lanes as much as possible

2. Horizontally (number of processes involved). Look for ways to remove a step in the process.

By shortening the map in both horizontal and vertical directions, you simplify the process, and thus making it more efficient.

Reduce Vertical swim lanes Crossed

The goal of reducing swim lanes is to simplify and reduce the number of people and groups involved in the process. The ideal process would have one swim lane, one person, and one step.

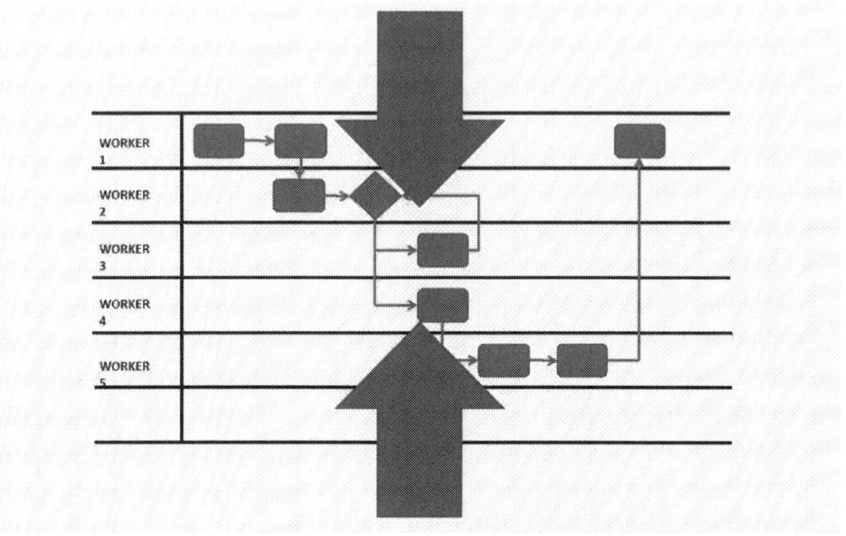

Figure 15.3 Process Map Compressed Vertically

Examine Repeat Touches

Identify where the product leaves and later returns to the same swim lane (person responsible). Meaning, the product goes from Joe to Mary, then back to Joe. Find out the reason why a worker has to touch the product twice, and eliminate where possible.

Examine Decision Rights

Extending decision-making rights can lead to HUGE opportunities to improve processes. While you analyze your process map, consider decision-rights and how changing the existing decision-rights can reduce the number of swim lanes crossed. Let me give you an example. Frequently a process crosses a swim lane for the sole purpose of supervisor approval, i.e. the worker submits a training request to a supervisor for approval. Though supervisor approvals add accountability they can often be huge time wasters, and add questionable value. Too often the supervisor does not examine the work product and blindly approves it. In this instance, crossing the swim lane to obtain the approval does not add value to the product. The easy choice is to reprimand the supervisor for blindly approving work products, but I'd like to convince you that before you reprimand, examine if the approval is really needed. The goal is to look for ways to add value to the product. The fewer swim lanes you cross the faster the product gets through the process.

Don't get me wrong, there is real value in accountability (especially for government organizations), but it's possible to deliver both accountability *and* efficiency improvement if you work smarter. Here's how:

- Assign decision-rights (authority) to the worker at the current step, and let them employ their best judgement, or instead,
- Outline the decision criteria the supervisor uses in making the decision to authorize/deny (such as sufficient funding, within policy, within scope, within schedule, etc.), and let the worker use that criterion to make the decision herself. This improvement saves time and simplifies the process by eliminating crossing into the supervisor swim lane, yet still maintains strong accountability

Does this make sense? Let me offer some examples. Consider giving the worker the decision authority to:

- Purchase items under a certain dollar amount
- Authorize a training request if no overnight hotel stay is needed
- Reduce defects by allowing the worker to stop processing if the quality is not up to standard

Reduce Horizontal Process Steps

Examine Useless Steps- identify the value of each step in the process and ask if that step is a 'need-to-have', a 'nice-to-have', 'redundant' or 'not needed'. Eliminate or shorten steps when possible. The ideal process would have one swim lane, one person, and one step.

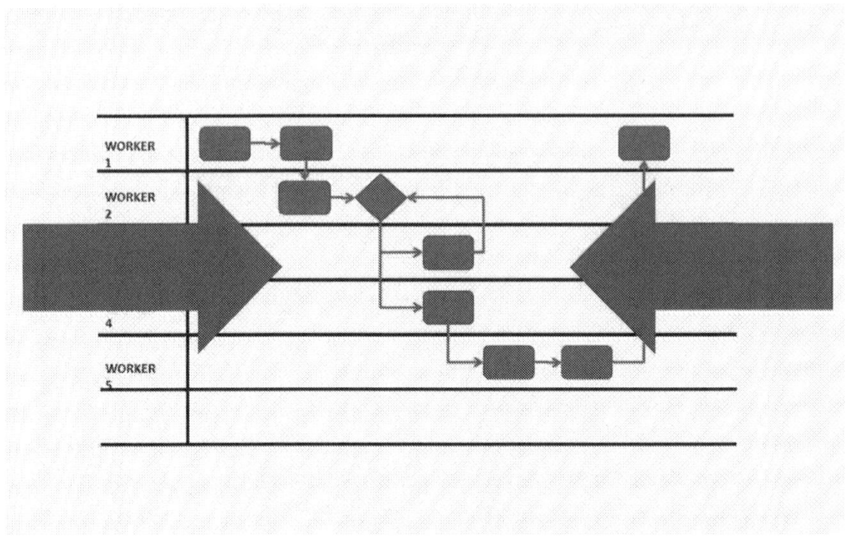

Figure 15.4 - Process Map Compressed Horizontally

Examine Step Order- identify if the order of the step makes logical sense for your work product. For example, do workers box an item then later unbox it to record a serial number?

Speaking of step order, let me ask you, why do online job applications collect so much in-depth personal history data (date of birth, social security number) that takes hours to complete and present data security issues when the candidate is not on the short list of candidates to interview (which is my #2 personal pet peeve). (My #1 pet peeve is left lane drivers,...but I digress).

Examine for Concurrency – identify if two steps can occur at the same time. This is a good thing for efficiency! Like how a convict can serve two sentences at the same time.

Examine for Batching - Batching is sometimes good, and other times it's bad. Batching is like Spiderman's powers, they can be helpful or harmful.

Identify if you have products waiting to be processed. In this instance, batching (waiting) is bad. Look for ways to eliminate 'waiting' before the next step. Seek to alter processes or technologies to eliminate or reduce wait times (sometimes called continuous flow manufacturing). The ideal is to continue to process a single product as soon as the product completes its last step (ideally a batch of 1). Examine why each product cannot continue to be processed individually. What's the hold up? Look for ways to update processes and technologies to reduce or eliminate batching (a.k.a. buffering).

That being said, batching can be a good choice if your technology and processes are more efficient with it.

For example, at the grocery store you don't get a gallon of milk, run to the checkout counter and pay; then run back and get a box of cereal, run to the checkout counter and pay, and do this for each item on your grocery list. That would be silly and a waste of time running back and forth with no added value. Instead, you batch all your groceries in your cart, then with a full cart, stroll to the checkout counter, and pay once.

Reduce Wait Time

Let's use grocery shopping as an example to look for opportunities to reduce wait time:

- eliminate the waiting in line to check out
- eliminate waiting while the checkout clerk scans each item
- eliminate wait time and manpower to bag the groceries

To reduce these wait times, my grocery store employs portable hand scanners for the shopper to scan the item UPC code as they place each item in their cart, into a recyclable shopping bag (scanning and bagging time reduced!). When done shopping, the shopper goes to a self-service checkout counter and pays the final bill (waiting in line reduced!). Bazinga! All three wait times are now reduced or eliminated. Families can now get home in time for the Sunday football game on TV.

REMEMBER, THE GOAL IS TO GET TO A BATCH SIZE OF 1!

In summary, BPR and process mapping should be used annually on every business process to find out how the process can be made ever more efficient, less costly, faster, or more effective.

Author's Note: Frequently, BPR analysis uncovers an inefficiency that a technology device or software product can make more efficient. Which is the purpose of a technology system, right,...to help the Power Leader do things better? The new technology should enable the Power Leader to do new things in better ways, or perhaps enable the Power Leader to stop doing things inefficiently the way they used to do them. Either way, the method of how the Power Leader works will change; and Power Leader will have to communicate these changes to employees (we'll cover change management later in the Communications and Transformation chapters later).

Now You Try It

Use the below blank process map and craft a process map for your project.

Which business process will you analyze and why?

____

____

____

____

Which SMEs will you interview to gather details and data?

____

____

What questions will you ask?

WORKER 1	WORKER 2	WORKER 3	WORKER 4	WORKER 5	WORKER 5

Root Cause Analysis

Chapter 16

Root Cause Analysis (RCA) helps you identify and troubleshoot performance bottlenecks, and the true causes of an issue. It works closely with process mapping technique See that chapter on process maps).

Objectives When you complete Chapter 16, you will be able to: • To identify performance bottlenecks and the root cause of issues, and not just its signs and symptoms	**Terms** • RCA • Bottleneck • DMAIC

RCA is the same process that doctors and nurses go through to diagnose a medical issue. But, RCA is more than just troubleshooting. Troubleshooting finds 'a' cause, while RCA helps you find 'the' cause. Repeat that last sentence to make sure you grasp the difference. It helps an administrator determine the true cause of an issue, and not just fix its indicators.

RCA HELPS YOU FIND 'THE' CAUSE

Auto mechanics, software coders, and nurse practitioners know what I'm talking about. Would you rather keep applying poison ivy itch relief cream, or would you rather not stand in a patch of poison ivy in the first place?

If you don't conduct root cause analysis, your bottlenecks will keep reappearing, and you process might fail just when you need it most; or you might spend time and resources fixing the wrong issue.

While you may find a single root cause, usually you discover there are several key contributing causes to the failure- called a systems failure. So, try to look for causes in each of five systems performance areas- people, policy, process, technology, and environment.

RCA uses a step-by-step approach called DMAIC. Define, Measure, Analyze, Improve, Control (DMAIC). DMAIC was developed by Deming during the 1950s. It's a statistical and analytical method used to reduce defects by uncovering their root causes, and fixing them.

Here's a guide to help you find the root cause(s) of you issue, using the DMAIC approach:

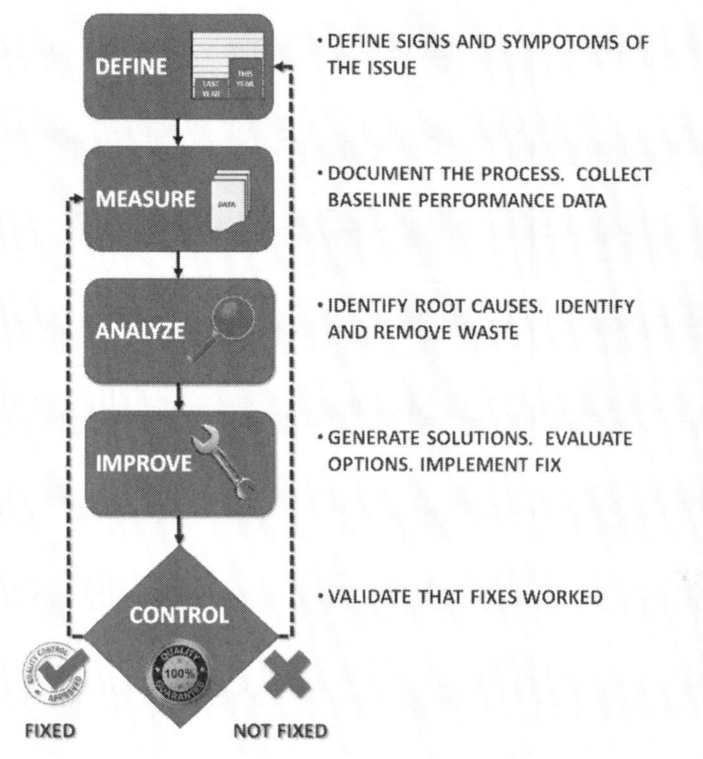

Figure 16.1 - DEMMING'S DMAIC Improvement cycle

DEFINE THE PROBLEM

What signs and symptoms indicate that there is a problem? In medical terms, what symptoms do the workers tell you; and what observable signs do you see? Example, lots of overtime used; high volume of citizen complaints; staff confusion and frustration; employee behavior problems, etc.

Beware, it's possible that the problem is not actually a real *problem*, but instead is a perceived problem. That's why we measure data points, in the next section. If after measuring data points, you find that processes and performance are occurring according to standards, then you can stop the DMAIC cycle now, because the problem is no more. However, in such a case you definitely have a communications problem that you'll need to address. Because for many, perception is reality, and perception left uncorrected can grow into morale problems and productivity loss.

MEASURE DATA POINTS

Gather performance data and collect examples of the issues you observe. Gather this info from technology sources (databases, spreadsheets, feedback records, etc.), and especially from personal interviews of both the supplier and the consumer of your business processes. The interviews of workers closest to the actual work are essential and give context to the data you collect…that senior management might otherwise not be aware of. Try to develop unbiased data to analyze. What workers 'feel' is important to capture, but often it can be misleading. Instead, gather as factual and unbiased data as possible.

ANALYZE POTENTIAL CAUSES

Analyze the data for trends, patterns, and anomalies, focusing on frequency of occurrences. Look for the key issue among all the issues; the most frequent person involved; most frequent day of the week, etc. Look at people, policy, process, technology, and environment.

THE 5X CAUSE

Now for the secret recipe- the 5x cause! The data gathering and analysis work that you just performed clue you into a key cause. Let's call it Cause-1. Now, ask yourself what causes Cause-1? The answer is Cause-2. Then ask what causes Cause-2. The answer is Cause-3. Repeat this question-answer routine two more times until you reach Cause-5. This becomes you root cause.

IMPROVE AND APPLY FIXES

Now that you have identified you root cause (Cause-5), it's time to implement your fixes. The best fixes occurs up-stream (earlier in the process) of all the other causes. But keep in mind that Cause-4 or Cause-3 might be less expensive, or easier to apply a fix to. That's okay. Go for it.

CONTROL FOR QUALITY

Did the fix work? Collect more data and check. Compare your findings to the data you collected when troubleshooting the problem. Was there a favorable change in the identified problem?

If the problem is not fixed, then start the cycle over with clarifying and confirming the signs and symptoms.

If the problem is fixed. Hooray! Tea and medals for everyone. Now put a quality assurance process in place to ensure it stays fixed, and to alert you when it starts to get out of balance again.

DMAIC EXAMPLE

Let's work through an RCA example of excessive overtime consumption, using the DMAIC approach:

- Define the Problem: You sense that overtime consumption is high. You check the monthly financials and determine that compared to standards (or last year) there is confirmed excessive overtime use. The easy/quick (and incorrect) solution would be to add more overtime funds and call it a day. But the Power Leader goes further and examines the causes of the overtime.
- Measure Data Points: Collect timesheet reports for the past 3 years for all relevant employees. Interview workers who claimed overtime.
- Analyze Causes five times (5x):
    1. What is causing overtime consumption?

- Identify key events that could have triggered the consumption. Analyze timesheet reports and discover that day shift employees (6am-6pm) consume a significantly higher amount of overtime compared to evening shift workers.

2. Why does day shift experience this increase?
    - Timesheet reports indicate workers can't complete paperwork before the end of their shift (6pm)

Interviewed supervisors and workers for their observations

3. Why can't workers complete paperwork by end of their shift?
    - Workers are still answering calls for service during their paperwork time (5pm-6pm), and policy requires paperwork to be completed by the end of shift

4. Why are workers too busy answering calls instead of completing their paperwork?
    - Not enough workers on duty to meet policy goal to respond to customer calls for service within 15 minutes (currently meeting 15 minute goal 82% of the time), and to complete paperwork at the same time

5. No need for a 5th question in this example. We have enough information to develop some promising solutions.

- Improve and Apply Fixes:

Our research shows that we can manipulate several processes to resolve the excessive overtime issue.

1. Schedule to have some evening workers adjust their shift two hours earlier (5pm-5am). This solution will increase day shift staffing levels during peak activity periods, without sacrificing evening shift workload that is lighter later in their shift (5am-6am).
2. Change policy to allow low-priority paperwork to be completed the next day during slow work periods.
3. Restructure performance goals- break customer service calls into high, medium, and low priority calls for service, and set different time response goals for each priority level. This will let the rights calls wait until the next shift comes on duty.

- Control for Quality: After one month activity, reviewed time sheet reports to discover overtime now reduced by 75%, and 15 minute response goal now up to 99%. Success!

By questioning several levels deep into the problem, you find the authentic cause of you issue, and by working smarter, you solutions significantly improved effectiveness and often saves an organization money!

Now You Try It

Identify a problem and use the DMAIC cycle to solve it.

DEFINE - (Define signs and sympotoms of the issue)

____

____

____

____

____

MEASURE - (Document the process. Collect baseline performance data)

____

____

____

____

____

ANALYZE - (Identify root causes. Identify and remove waste)

____

____

____

____

____

IMPROVE - (Generate solutions. Evaluate options.)

____

____

____

____

____

CONTROL - (Validate fixes)

____

____

____

____

____

Identify the Good, the Bad, and the Ugly

Chapter 17

Want to find out the good, the bad, and the ugly of your organization? You need S.W.O.T. S.W.O.T. are <u>not</u> tactical police officers wearing black, armed with M4 assault rifles, and rappelling from the tops of skyscrapers- that's S.W.**<u>A</u>**.T. We're talking about S.W.**<u>O</u>**.T.- the study of an organization's internal <u>Strengths</u> and <u>Weaknesses</u>, and its external <u>Opportunities</u> and <u>Threats</u>.

Objectives When you complete Chapter 17, you will be able to: • To deliver a condensed 360° picture of the health of you organization	**Terms** • SWOT • Force Field Analysis • Gap Analysis

A SWOT analysis is usually presented in the form of a quad chart....but this time it really does have only four quadrants.

SWOT is a condensed version of describing what's good and what's bad about you organization. SWOT gives you situational awareness of your organization, so you can make effective decisions; and it's a great kick-starter to craft effective strategies for growth and change.

If you don't add SWOT analysis to your tool kit and regularly review your organization with one, your organization could be flying blind and subject to crashing. You will struggle with your decision making and strategic planning efforts. You will likely miss key threats to you program's survival.

SWOT's situational analysis can be used on any number of topics- from improving your business, exploring new initiatives, making decisions about new policies, identifying possible areas for change.

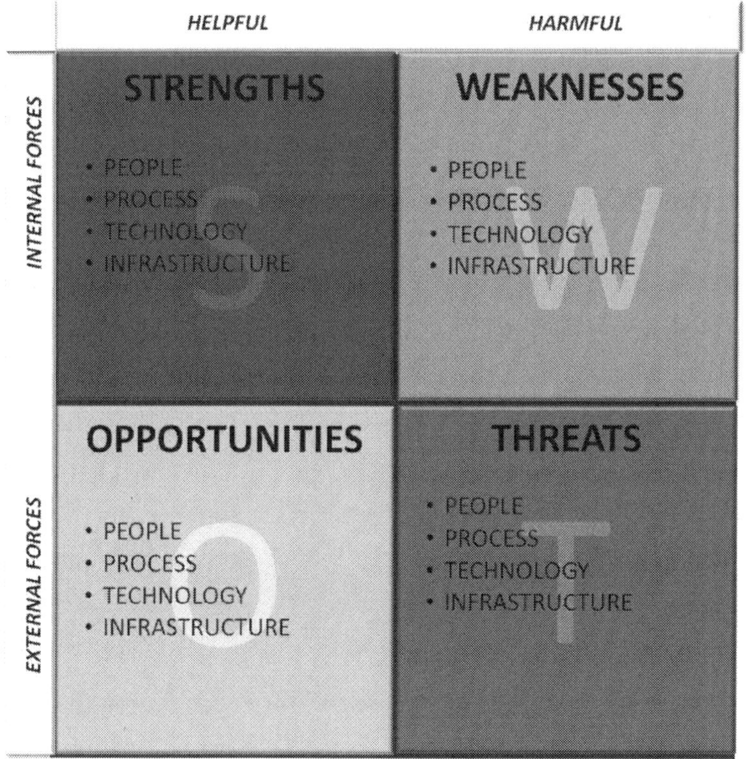

Figure 17.1 - SWOT Quad chart

Think about a personal use for SWOT, for example, a situation where your boss invites you to join her for lunch. I bet you execute a simplified SWOT analysis in your head:

- Strengths- your business unit has been performing well recently

- Weaknesses- you were 10 minutes late to a meeting this morning
- Opportunities- face-time with the boss to discuss your new ideas
- Threats- You may not make it back in time for you next meeting, and she may want to talk to you about promptness

Given this info about you situation, do you accept the boss's lunch invitation? Just for the record, *always* accept your boss's invitation to lunch!

The output of a SWOT analysis is a 'quad chart'. The quad chart can serve many purposes when you want to communicate about your project or program:

- Give a quick overall view of the state of you organization or project
- Provide focus and direction to kick start you strategic planning discussions. When I say strategic planning, I also mean decision making.
- Helps you understand and document what you organization does well and what separates you from competitors (**strengths**)
- Helps you understand and document the areas you are currently vulnerable to business collapse, program shutdown, project failure, etc. (**weaknesses**)
- Helps you document and keep abreast of trends and upcoming changes in you environment (**opportunities**)
- Warns you of and documents impending harm to you organization (**threats**)

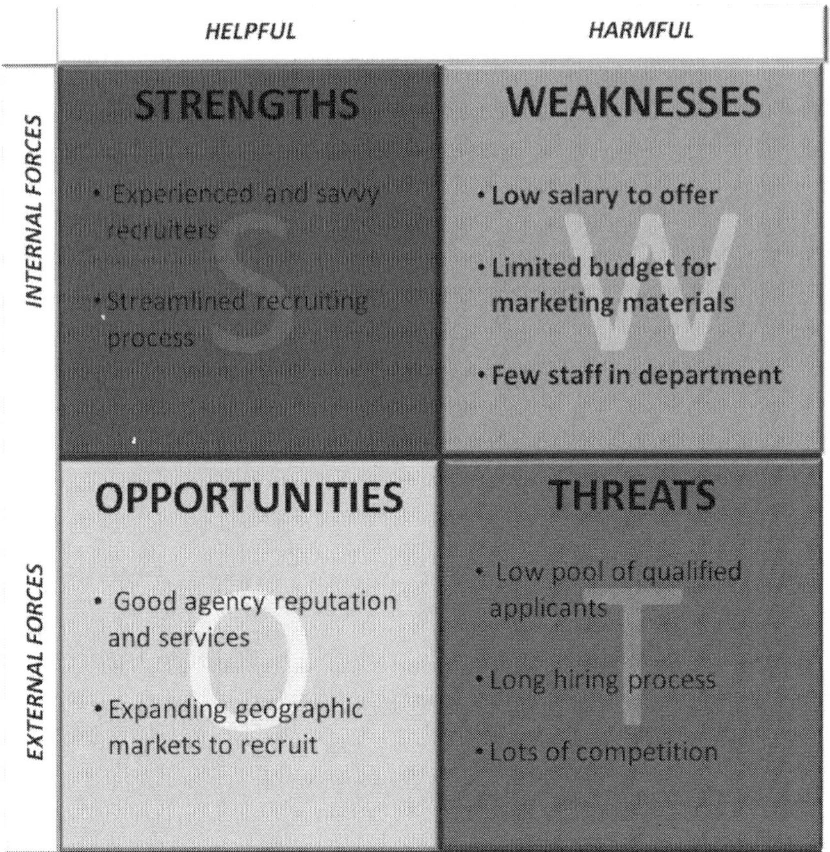

Figure 20 Example SWOT for a Recruiting Unit

When you think of strengths, weaknesses, opportunities, and threats, consider looking for them in multiple performance areas- people, policy, process, technology, environment, funding, safety, political influence, reputation, and other themes valuable to you organization.

For example, let's consider the status of a human resources recruiting unit. After the SWOT analysis, we'll use it to develop strategies to capitalize on the positives, and to reduce the impact of the negatives.

How to Use a S.W.O.T. Chart

Now that your SWOT quad chart is complete, what do you do with it? SWOT analysis is a precursor to the strategic planning process. Given the SWOT perspective of your organization, you refer to it to help identify directions you want your organization to grow in. From the direction, create S.M.A.R.T. goals and associated strategies to target and reduce the impact of the weaknesses and threats; and to target and take advantage of your strengths and opportunities. See the chapter on strategic planning.

- Match Strengths with Opportunities
- Convert Weaknesses into Strengths

From this SWOT example, you might consider the below strategies:

- Develop a document containing three innovative recruitment strategies the recruitment unit wants to try
- Develop marketing materials that showcase the agency reputation and services
- Authorize recruitment in extended geographic areas
- Alter earliest promotion schedule or offer sign-on bonus
- Authorize temporary recruiting staff during a sprint
- Reconsider acceptable dress code, tattoo restrictions, education requirements
- Conduct business process reengineering effort to make recruitment cycle more efficient

Key words:

- *Force Field analysis* - takes SWOT analysis a step further by identifying the forces driving or hindering change—in other words, the forces driving its strengths, weaknesses, opportunities, and threats
- *Gap analysis* - used gap analysis to measure the quality

Now You Try It

Craft a S.W.O.T. analysis on your business unit:

	HELPFUL	*HARMFUL*
INTERNAL FORCES	**STRENGTHS** S	**WEAKNESSES** W
EXTERNAL FORCES	**OPPORTUNITIES** O	**THREATS** T

Given your SWOT analysis, come up with a plan to take advantage of you strengths and opportunities; and a plan to reduce you threats and weaknesses.

How will you match Strengths with Opportunities?

How will you convert Weaknesses into Strengths?

Performance Metrics

Chapter 18

Performance Metrics are the work activity we'll count and measure so we can tell if our performance is achieving our goals. For example, we count the number of permits issued; we count the response time for fire departments; we count the parts per million of water sanitary levels; we count the dollar amount of tax collected; etc.

Objectives When you complete Chapter 18, you will be able to: • To determine the right performance metrics to capture, and how to use them to manage and improve your work	**Terms** • Metric • Baseline Throughput • Input • Output • Outcome

WHAT IS A METRIC?

So then, what's a *metric*? A metric is the thing we count or measure that will inform us how well we perform. In baseball terms, its batting average. In financial terms, it's the DOW average. In retail, it could be average customer wait time. In manufacturing, it could be defects per thousand. In government, it could be citizen satisfaction levels, counting the number of applications processed, or number of workers achieving certification.

What is Baseline Throughput?

Along with a performance metric, an administrator also needs to understand the acceptable standard that the work activity should meet. This is called the baseline throughput. In other words, did the work hit the mark?

A smart Power Leader tracks the *right* work activity to measure; and defines a desired *baseline* throughput goal; and she monitors and *reports* how the measurement varies from expected standards.

Why measure performance?

How does a ship's captain know the health status of his ship? He can't be everywhere at once. He must rely on regular status reporting from all of his ship's sections- engine room, weapons, navigation, and sick bay. Remember from the Star Trek TV how the pretty female crewman would bring Captain Kirk the "iPad" for him to review and sign off on? In the same way, how do you know if an organization is healthy and performing well; or if it's rusting under the surface? Answer, you create the right performance metrics and regularly report on them.

MEASURE PERFORMANCE AND REGULARLY REPORT

Like Captain Kirk (Piccard, et. Al.) the smart administrator implements regular status reporting to determine if workers' performance is meeting (or not meeting) expectations & goals, so he can reward workers, or take steps to mitigate the issues.

Report by Exception Is Bad

Unfortunately, status reporting in many organizations relies on reporting by 'exception'. By 'exception' I mean that the boss doesn't receive regular reporting on the performance of his business units, until something bad happens. He takes the approach that no news is good news- that silence is good. That if no one complains, then everything must be good, and he can concentrate on other matters. It's a reactive method of managing and, really, it's not managing at all.

Manage Proactively

On the other hand, proactive management with regular reporting takes effort and yields great value. A proactively managed organization is much more effective and prevents issues from becoming problems. By becoming aware of our performance, we can assess how healthy our organization is; and make adjustments to improve the outcome of the work.

Report Performance

But, how can the Power Leader fix this shortfall and turn a reactive organization into a proactive one? One that can identify issues before they become problems. One that can warn you before work quality and productivity begin to suffer. One that can reveal where resources should be re-deployed. One that helps the Power Leader to build a bullet-proof case to justify the need for increased staff, bigger budget, and more resources.

The answer – Performance Reporting:

1) Establish the right performance metrics, and
2) Define a baseline goal of work throughput, and
3) Deliver regular performance reporting, as part of a larger performance management strategy. Compare the performance to the baseline to see how well you're doing

When we talk about work *performance* we really mean how well does our work throughput and quality compare to our expected standards or policy? If the output matches or exceeds our expectations, then we are performing well.

Remember to also include performance metrics that measure *quality* as part of your entire performance management reporting. It's equally important to measure the *quantity* of the thing you produce and to measure the *quality* of the products/services that you produce.

MEASURE PERFORMANCE WITH METRICS

CASE STUDY EXAMPLE

To discover which meaningful performance metrics to collect, measure, and report on, look at your mission statement. For this case study, let's review the mission statement of the Washington D.C. Department of Human Resources (DCHR) for possible metrics:

> *"The DC Department of Human Resources (DCHR) provides human resource management services that strengthen individual and organizational performance and enable the District government to attract, develop and retain a well-qualified, diverse workforce."*

Some potential performance measures jump right out-

- Services that strengthen the individual
- Services that strengthen the organization
- Services to attract
- Services to develop
- Services to retain
- Diversity

Services that strengthen the individual

Let's define this statement to be about keeping the worker informed of departmental concerns, ensure fair labor practices, create educational opportunities, etc. So, an outcome measure could be- the awareness level of employees for the offered programs.

Services that strengthen the organization

Let's define this statement to be about filling all open positions, so the agency can perform at its optimum. So, an outcome measure could be- the percentage of positions filled, compared to all positions (otherwise known as vacancy rate).

Services that attract [workers]
Let's define this statement to be about a large enough pool of candidates from which to choose, for each position. So, an outcome measure could be- the average number of qualified candidates per position that are above a minimum threshold (5-6 qualified candidates per position).

Services that develop [workers]
Let's define this statement to be about training and educating the worker to be able to perform at a peak level. So, an outcome measure could be- the percentage of workers who received a new skill or capability.

Services that retain [workers]
Let's define this statement to be about enticing employees to remain working for the organization. So, an outcome measure could be- the turnover rate of employees, expressed as a percentage (a.k.a. churn).

Diversity
Let's define this statement to be about enabling equal employment opportunity for different races, religions, genders, ages, etc. So, an outcome measure could be- the percentage of each diversity group as it relates to the total worker population.

WORK INPUT, OUTPUT, OUTCOME

Okay, so you decide to measure your work activity. Let's make sure you measure the right kind of work activity. Consider three options to create the right metrics- specifically work *input*, work *output;* and how they are not as meaningful as work *outcome*.

Many government agencies deceptively link performance success with activity *input*- how many people or hours were applied to an issue. Equally imperfect, agencies measure *output*- how many fines were levied, or how many inspections were conducted, or how many people reached. While these *output* metrics are easy to count, frequently they aren't very helpful to inform us how well the organization is achieving its goal. Instead, the Power Leader could seek to measure outcome (observed changes to the issue).

To examine the difference between input, output, and outcome, let's consider a neighborhood problem of illegally parked cars:

Work *input* is assigning two officers to work for two hours on writing parking tickets. Sadly, the numbers of hours worked doesn't tell us if we are solving the key problem of illegally parked cars.

Work *output* is counting the number of parking tickets the officers issued. But don't be fooled. Counting the number of tickets issued doesn't tell us if we are solving the key problem of illegally parked cars. Think about it, with some innovation, you could solve the problem without issuing any parking tickets at all. For example, Police agencies could deploy mobile sign boards to educate the public, install better signage, or install parking meters, etc.

The best metric to choose directly corresponds to the mission goal. In this case, define mission success with counting the number of illegally parked cars- before, and then after resolution efforts. In other words, measure the *outcome* of observing fewer illegally parked cars. This metric directly informs us if we are solving the key problem of illegally parked cars

NOTE: Your agency could choose to report to the public on input and output measures. However, the more authentic and meaningful measure is to report outcome.

RATIO METRICS ARE BEST

Whether you measure input, output, or outcome, reporting on raw data doesn't give context or meaning to the numbers; for example, 35 permits; 6 minutes response, 18 overtime hours, etc. These numbers don't tell us anything about how well we are performing. Instead, let's explore an array of metric reporting options (raw, ration, TYLY, percent), and see if we can understand what each option delivers.

Raw Metrics (not valuable)
Raw metrics are simply reporting on the counting of widgets produced. These are not valuable.

	COUNTS
	THIS YEAR
PERMITS PROCESSED	562
OFFICE CLERKS	3
COMMUNITY POPULATION	185,000

Figure 18.1 Raw Metrics (not valuable without context)

For example, what does 562 business license permits processed mean? Is that a high number or a low number? Did the number of permits issued solve the problem of illegal businesses? Raw metrics offer little value because they lack context and meaning.

Ratio Metrics

Perhaps the best and most meaningful performance metrics are *ratio* metrics ('something' per 'something else'). For example, average permits processed *per* worker; or hours *per* building inspection; or cost *per* training hour.

The two benefits of ratio metrics are they:

- *Normalize* (scale) your data, so you can fairly compare apples to apples performance across different time periods, or across different agencies with different numbers of staff or population, etc.
- Deliver more insight and context into performance, than counting outputs alone

	COUNTS			
	LAST YEAR	THIS YEAR	CHANGE	OUTCOME
PERMITS PROCESSED	418	562	+34%	INCREASE
OFFICE CLERKS	3	3	+0%	NO CHANGE
COMMUNITY POPULATION	160,000	185,000	+16%	INCREASE
AVG PERMITS *PER* WORKER	139	187	+34.4%	INCREASE
1 PERMIT *PER* 'N' RESIDENTS	383	329	-14.0%	DECREASE
1 CLERK *PER* 'N' RESIDENTS	53,333	61,667	+15.6%	INCREASE

Figure 18.2 - Ratio Metrics - 'Something per Something Else'

In this example, (see figure 18.2) three useful ratio metrics are 'average number of permits per worker'; 'one permit issued for every n resident'; 'one clerk available to service n number of residents'.

By comparing ratio values, you can assess performance fairly and accurately, because ratios automatically re-scale and adjust for changes in the number of clerks, permits, or population, etc.

So, what new intelligence do the ratio metrics give us that we couldn't get from raw or percent alone?

- 562 - The raw number of permits processed. Doesn't tell us anything.
- 144 – Increase in permits. Tells us the direction of change (increase or decrease), but doesn't reveal the strength if the change (increase a lot or a little?)
- 34% - Percentage increase in permit applications. Tells us that we had a strong increase in the number of permit applications.
- -14% - Tells us that even though the population is increasing, fewer residents are applying for permits.

Analysis - Notice that while the number of permit applications have increased (34%), it is likely due to the increase in population. So, you might consider adding more clerks to meet the increased demand. However, the <u>rate of the increase</u> is slowing (a negative 14%); so if you choose to hire more clerks, you may wish to hire fewer than what you may have thought, and let time reduce the number of permits.

This Year vs Last Year Metrics (TYLY)

Another metric to consider is to report on performance during comparative time periods- *this* year compared to *last* year, or maybe *this* month vs *last* month, or *this* quarter vs *last* quarter.

	COUNTS			
	LAST YEAR	THIS YEAR	CHANGE	OUTCOME
PERMITS PROCESSED	418	562	+144	INCREASE
OFFICE CLERKS	3	3	+0	NO CHANGE
COMMUNITY POPULATION	160,000	185,000	+25,000	INCREASE

Figure 18.3 - TYLY Metrics

A rudimentary analysis of the TYLY tell us that this year, office clerks processed 144 more permits than last year, and the community population grew by 25,000 people....but so what? Is the increase in permits okay, or should the agency do something, like add more office clerks? What does the current population value tell us? Not much.

TYLY metrics are very good and could be included in most reporting. They reveal trends, but are not fully informative by themselves.

Percent Change Metrics

Another consideration is to take the TYLY raw number change (see figure 18.3) and convert it to a *percentage* change. Using a percentage change compares the current values to historical values, and tells us the amplitude (strength) of the change. This percentage context yields better intelligence and insight into our performance.

	COUNTS			
	LAST YEAR	THIS YEAR	CHANGE	OUTCOME
PERMITS PROCESSED	418	562	+34%	INCREASE
OFFICE CLERKS	3	3	+0%	NO CHANGE
COMMUNITY POPULATION	160,000	185,000	+16%	INCREASE

Figure 18.4 - Percent Metrics

You see, a change of 144 more permits doesn't tell us much. Is 144 good or bad? Manageable or not manageable? But representing the same change in terms of a percentage (+34% increase), tells us much more, specifically how strong the change is.

MONTHLY PERFORMANCE REPORT

So, now that you've identified what work activity to measure (input, output, outcome), and you've defined which format to present the information (raw, TYLY, percentage, ratio); the only thing left is to compile the info into a report and deliver it to your boss and team to review discuss next steps.

In summary, a smart Power Leader tracks the *right* work activity to measure; defines a desired *baseline* throughput goal; and she monitors and *reports* how the measurement varies from expected values.

Tip: Sometimes your data is so large or damaged that you can't measure the entire population. Instead, consider taking representative samples from your data, then measure and report on those.

NOW YOU TRY IT

Develop three <u>new</u> mission performance metrics? For each, define what these metrics measure- input, output, or outcome?

____

____

____

____

____

____

____

____

____

For any <u>existing</u> metrics, how could you change them to be ratios?

____

____

____

____

____

Communicate to Persuade

Chapter 19

Getting more resources for your project or program can be difficult. Here's how to get your request to be the most compelling and win your resources!

Objectives When you complete Chapter 19, you will be able to: • to make a compelling argument for your resource request	**Terms** • Resource • Data-Driven

First Work to Avoid the Resource Request

Better than requesting more resources, is to eliminate the need for them in the first place. Before any resource request, the smart Power Leader meets with her team, evaluates her program performance and processes, and discusses options for becoming more efficient. The first option should always be to look for opportunities to increase efficiency and re-engineer your business processes.

LOOK FIRST TO IMPROVE EFFICIENCY

For example, consider a building inspection department that experiences an increase in building inspection requests- from an average of 6 inspections per inspector per day, to 7 inspections per inspector, per day. A rise of 14%! Use your new-found skills and see if you can find efficiency improvements. See the chapters on Business Process Re-engineering, and Root Cause Analysis, and Process Maps.

THE REQUEST CONTENT

When it finally comes down to a request for more resources, frequently program managers tell their executives that they need more staffing or other resources, but can't provide evidence-based (data-driven) proof why they need more, or how much more they need. Sadly, they rely on communicating feelings and judgements to express that they need more resources. This approach doesn't work. Executives don't care about your feelings; instead they need data-driven evidence to persuade them, and so they can justify their allocation of resources to others (the public).

THE LANGUAGE

Top level business executives speak a language of their own and are best persuaded on issues that affect them, so communicate in terms of their interests, and in a language they understand.

So what language do they understand and thus need to hear? Shape your resource request argument in:

- Deviation from standards
- Political terms
- Financial terms
- Program outcome terms
- Risk terms

Deviation from a Standard

Select the right metric (a ratio metric preferably) that fairly describes how your current workload is outside of policy or baseline standards. Your boss may press back and say your performance is not sufficient, and that's where you step in and present your previous efficiency improvements and how you've already stretched as far as you can go.

To explain, consider the ideal work throughput for a building inspection department. Work throughput is how much work you can do in a given time period. To estimate what the baseline throughput should be, find the maximum work hours possible in one day, and the total amount of work to be accomplished in that work day.

- There are 7.5 work hours in a day (with half-hour lunch)
- It takes 1.25 hours to complete 1 inspection

Therefore, a throughput standard should be for each inspector to conduct 6 inspections per day:

7.5 work hours = 6 inspections x 1hr 15 min

But what if inspection requests increased to 7 inspections per day? That means each inspection must be completed 11 minutes quicker (in 1hr 4 min vs 1hr 15 min).

If you can't come up with efficiency improvements, then your choices for a response without more resources become limited. Here are some alternative solutions (in no particular order) along with their effects.

- Consume overtime to allow a full inspection period
    - and burn up your budget before year end
    - and possibly burn out your team
- Reduce the inspection time per inspection
    - and possibly decrease quality
    - and possibly miss a safety issue
- Revert back to 6 inspections standard and create a backlog of inspections
    - and not meet public demand and expectations
- Ask for a mid-year budget increase and authorization to hire another inspector
    - and this will take time

Political Terms

Politics play a role in every work and social situation. So, research the political and social environment of your resource supplier (your boss, or whoever grants you the resources). What political and social issues do they face? Craft your argument in terms that will place them into a better political or social position. Think in terms of a positive press release to the public (through news media, or social network)

For example, communicate the idea that if the government administrator authorizes one additional inspector to the building inspection department, then they could soon put out a press release that the organization (and by proxy its leadership) continue to meet community expectations. The outcome of your resource is positive social capitol for your boss.

Financial Terms

Communicate the financial impact of your resource proposal. Communicate it in terms of the input dollars; the dollar value of the outcome; the dollar value of the ongoing operations & maintenance costs; and remember to add the dollar value *loss* if you don't receive your resource request.

For example, communicate the idea that if the government administrator authorizes an additional $500k to fund crisis intervention training for police officers, then they will be better prepared to respond to crisis events. The outcome in dollar terms is priceless (lives saved). The operations and maintenance costs are a fraction of the initial training. The costs of not adequately responding to such an event are exorbitant, and likely greater than the training request costs (lawsuits, bad press, loss of public confidence, etc.).

Program Outcome Terms

Communicate the program effectiveness gain if your resources are granted. For example, communicate the idea that if the government administrator authorizes the additional funding or manpower, that you could improve program success by 23%. See the chapter on Performance Metrics to figure out what to measure to show program effectiveness.

Risk Terms

Explain the likely and possible risks involved in the resource request. Be sure to highlight what bad things will happen if the organization does not supply the resources. This is called the 'burning platform'. Have bullet points ready so your boss can use them if she needs to persuade someone else.

THE REQUEST STRUCTURE

Now that we've outlined some things to bring up in your resource request document, let's discuss how best to arrange the request on paper. This should look familiar to you. Use a similar format to the one used in how to create a whitepaper. See the chapter on how to write a Whitepaper.

LANDSCAPE SECTION

Describe the current landscape of how things are today. Describe what's in place, how many workers, the baseline standards, etc.

CHALLENGE SECTION

Describe the problem, the workload, the deviation from standards, quality measures, how much time it takes to produce. Include future impacts (pop growth, office shut down, special event, new transportation system coming online, etc.). Show deviation from national or state standards, laws, regulations, policies. Add personal quotes when possible. Show how the world will burn if you don't get resources. Describe the burning platform if you don't get the resources.

STREAMLINED EFFORTS TO DATE SECTION

Present how your team has analyzed existing processes and practices and list what was done do to streamline efforts. This eliminates the question of "what can you do to become more efficient with existing resources".

For example, you conducted an organizational assessment and BPR effort and were able to find efficiencies that allowed you to make one more call-taker available to manage calls but that you still fall outside of national standards.

- List implemented efficiency 1
- List implemented efficiency 2
- List implemented efficiency 3

Solutions Section

Describe how more resources will resolve the problem. Describe exactly how much/many resources are needed. Consider giving an Option A, Option B, and Option C of what can be accomplished with different levels of resources.

This is where you go for the kill and ask for what you want. Present a list of options, and which option you recommend for budget approval. Explain the options in terms of costs and program outcome. Convert each solution to a dollar figure and a public satisfaction figure.

Risks Section

List the consequences and risks of each option. Explain their impact in terms of dollars and public satisfaction.

Nest Steps Section

Describe next steps

Graphics and Charts Are Key!

Adding graphics and charts to your resource document makes it more compelling and visually appealing. They convey a great amount of information in a little space.

TIP! Understand that a budget document is a political document, so understand that politics will be in play when discussing it.

NOW YOU TRY IT!

Consider the impact of standards, politics, finances, program, and risks surrounding your request.

What is your work throughput standard, and how has it deviated?

____

____

____

____

____

What political and social issues does your resource provider face? How will the resource request affect them?

____

____

____

____

____

Describe the financial impact of receiving the resources, and of not receiving the resources

____

____

____

____

Describe the program outcome changes if resources are granted, and if withheld

____

____

____

____

____

____

Outline your strategy to request more resources:

The Landscape (current environment/conditions)

____

____

____

____

____

The Challenge(s)

(Describe in terms of standards, political, financial, program, risks)

____

____

____

____

____

Streamlined Efforts to Date

Possible Solutions

(Describe in terms of standards, political, financial, program, risks)

Describe the risks of receiving or not receiving resources, and how you would mitigate those risks. (Describe in terms of standards, political, financial, program, risks)

Describe the next steps involved

____

____

____

____

____

____

Strategic Communications

Chapter 20

Get comfy, 'cause this is gonna be a long chapter. Next to Strategic Planning, Strategic Communications (stratcomm) is the most important management skill set. You keep seeing the word *strategic* in the labels of these skill-sets. That's because strategic means intentional and focused. When you are strategic, you are deliberate with your communications to achieve a specific desired outcome.

Objectives When you complete Chapter 20, you will be able to: • To use strategic communications as a tool to manage organizational change	**Terms** • Change Champion • Adoption Curve • Commitment Curve • Early Adopter

EMBRACE CHANGE

Strategic Communications is communicating the right message, to the right audience, at the right time, by the right medium, to control and manage organizational change. Its intended result is to win the hearts and minds of all workers so they embrace the change, rather than resist the change.

During any organizational change, there is always some level of uncertainty or anxiety that creates resistance to change; and it's your job to ensure you alleviate that anxiety and uncertainty to earn employee buy-in rather than resistance.

For example, consider a young married couple expecting a new baby. The couple experiences a certain level of anxiety and uncertainty if they have the skills needed to be good parents; if their home is large enough to accommodate an expanding family'; if they earn enough money to pay for childcare; if both parents can continue to work a full time job; etc. Having a first baby is a big change, right?

Applying the impact of change to a business environment, consider a government organization that plans to implement a new financial accounting system. At first glance you might think no big deal. But, for others it could be a change that affects their morale and work performance. Consider questions that workers might have- am I technology savvy enough to use it? Will it be difficult to learn? Will it give me the reporting that I need? What capability will I lose when we switch to the new system? How will it make my current work tasks more burdensome?

The smart administrator uses stratcomm to quell these concerns and stimulate worker buy-in so the organizational change happens smoothly without lowering morale, work productivity, or work quality.

The key takeaway is, if you don't underscore all your project work with good stratcomm, you're putting your change effort at risk for succeeding.

Before we get into how to conduct the stakeholder analysis, let's take a moment to talk about attitudes towards adoption of change (Adoption Curve), and how we could measure progress with change acceptance levels (Acceptance Curve).

THE CHANGE ADOPTION CURVE

To set your expectations, not everyone will agree and support your change initiatives. The Rogers Adoption Curve (Diffusion of Innovation (DOI) Theory, developed by E.M. Rogers in 1962) describes which groups of your workers will likely adopt your change first, second, etc.; and therefore which groups you should approach first. In other words, only a small select group of risk-takers will follow you at first (because their personality type welcomes change); followed by a bell curve of other groups (based on their attitudes towards change). The Rogers curve was intended to describe adoption of technologies, but it also applies to adopting change of any type.

This chart teaches us that we should first target our change efforts toward the Innovators. We should design our stratcomm on them as the target audience.

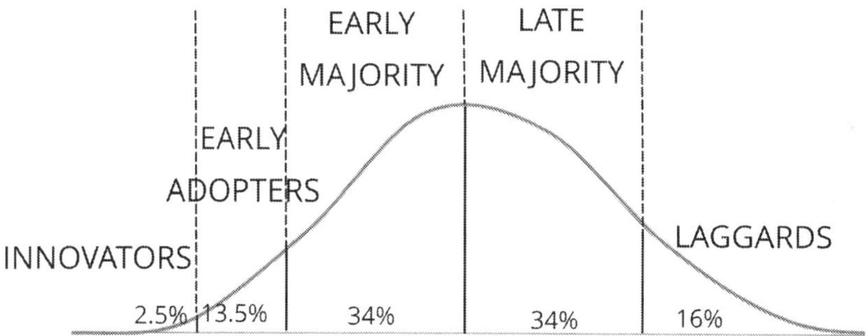

Figure 20.1 - Rogers Adoption Curve

The *Innovators* are the people who are more willing to try new things and gladly accept risk. These are the bleeding edge folks. The ones who wait in line all night to buy the next release of the iPhone. They love change and innovation.

These Innovators will immediately give you their support, and internalize your ideas quicker than others. You approach these people first. These are the people you want as your 'Change Champions'. They will help you gather support and buy-in from the other four groups.

The next acceptance group is the *Early Adopters*. These people are forward leaning and embrace smart change. These are the leading edge people who won't wait in line all night, but will upgrade their cell phones the moment they hit the stores. This is the next group you want to target with your messaging.

The next group is the *Early Majority*. These are the people who have seen proven success and know the acceptance momentum is building. These people are the largest group and welcome a new iPhone for Christmas or their birthday. This is the first of two largest groups to reach. Big gains will happen here.

The *Late Majority* are those people who are risk averse and reluctantly accept the change, but only after it has been well proven or seen as inevitable. They too share the top spot for the largest group of people to reach. These people figure they should probably move from a flip phone to an iPhone.

The *Laggards* are the final group to follow, if they follow at all. These folks are highly reluctant to change and will potentially try to sabotage your change effort. These are the 'I don't want a mobile phone' people. I've never focused much stratcomm efforts on this group. I've had to rely on performance management techniques to gain the buy-in from this crowd.

THE CHANGE COMMITMENT CURVE

Another curve you should be aware of is the Change Commitment Curve (adapted from Dr. Elisabeth Kübler-Ross, 1969, *On Death and Dying*). It describes the path people follow as they adjust to their changing environment. Your goal as a strategic communicator is to move people along this curve from Awareness to Internalization, as quickly and smoothly as possible.

Use the change curve to determine what the content of your messaging could be at different states of the organizational change.

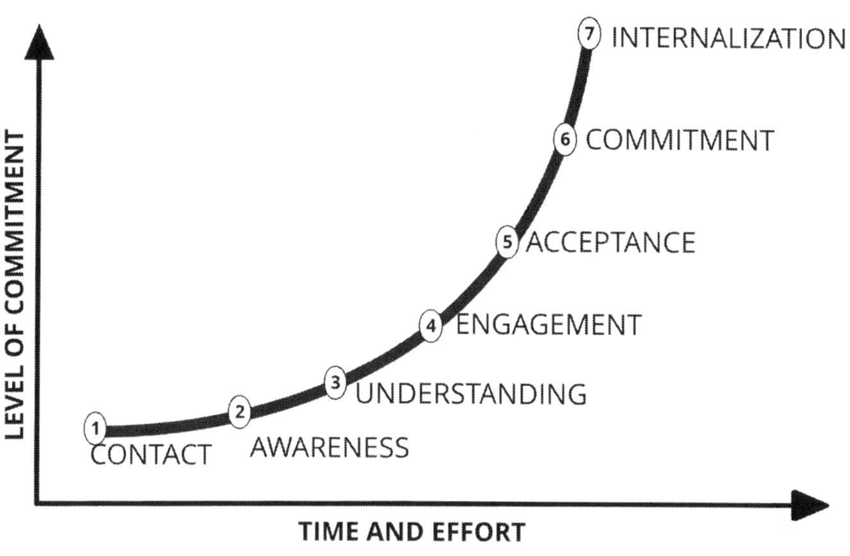

Figure 20.2 – Change Commitment Curve

Contact – workers first hear of a change coming in the organization, but can't explain what it is

Awareness – workers become aware of what the change is, and can describe it in simple terms

Understanding - workers realize that the change will affect them, and understand the reason for the change. They begin to ask questions.

Engagement – workers begin to reach out and ask about the project; they read the brochures, and pay attention to the communications pieces

Acceptance – workers realize that change is coming, despite their support or rejection of it.

Commitment – workers accept the change, perhaps preparing to accept it on their terms. Possibly they experiment with the new change.

Internalization – workers accept the new way of doing things. A new normal has been established.

Use these stages to measure how well your strategic communications strategies are working, and to assess the effectiveness of your overall change management program.

BUILD A COMMUNICATIONS PLAN

So let's create a stratcomm plan. It involves the following steps, begin with Identify Stakeholders.

1. Identify Stakeholders
2. Conduct Interviews
3. Identify Communications Mediums
4. Identify Messaging and Themes
5. Develop Communications Plan

IDENTIFY STAKEHOLDERS (STEP 1)

A *stakeholder* is any person who will be affected by, or who could influence the organizational change, regardless of how intensely the affect/impact is. Stakeholders can be CEOs, supervisors, workers, the public, suppliers, taxpayers, or anyone who can influence or be impacted by the change.

A *stakeholder analysis* is a research process that identifies the stakeholder groups, their level of impact by the change, their level of influence on the change, their current understanding of the change, what questions or concerns they have, and other related roadblocks to acceptance.

Stakeholder Analysis Matrix
This matrix is where you catalog all of your information about messaging. It is the chief source of information to guide you in your stratcomm plan- what to communicate, to whom, when, how often, etc. The product of a stakeholder analysis is a matrix.

There are a number of different matrix models to use, depending upon the complexity of your project. A simple quad matrix like figure 20.3, or a complex chart like figure 20.4.

High Influence/High Impact	Low Influence/High Impact
• Stakeholder A • Stakeholder B	• Stakeholder A • Stakeholder B
High Influence/Low Impact	**Low Influence/Low Impact**
• Stakeholder A • Stakeholder B	• Stakeholder A • Stakeholder B

Figure 20.3 – Simple Stakeholder Analysis Matrix

PROJECT: ALTER BUS ROUTES						
STAKEHOLDER NAME	IMPACT	INFLUENCE	WHAT IS IMPORTANT TO STAKEHOLDER?	HOW COULD THE STAKEHOLDER CONTRIBUTE TO THE PROJECT	HOW COULD HE STAKEHOLDER BLOCK THE PROJECT?	STRATEGY FOR ENGAGING THE STAKEHOLDER
SCHOOL BOARD	LOW	HIGH	PUBLIC ACCEPTANCE; RE-BALANCE BUS CAPACITY	RESOURCES	REFUSE RESOURCES	EQUIP MEMBERS WITH PROJECT STATUS AND REASON FOR CHANGE
PRINCIPALS	LOW	LOW	NOT AFFECTING OPERATIONS	RELAY COMMUNICATIONS	NEGATIVE COMMUNICATIONS	EDUCATE ON IMPORTANCE OF RELAYING COMMUNICATION; POSITIVE ATTITUDE
TEACHERS	LOW	LOW	NOT AFFECTING OPERATIONS	RELAY COMMUNICATIONS	NEGATIVE COMMUNICATIONS	EDUCATE ON IMPORTANCE OF RELAYING COMMUNICATION; POSITIVE ATTITUDE
STAFF	LOW	LOW	NOT AFFECTING OPERATIONS	RELAY COMMUNICATIONS	NEGATIVE COMMUNICATIONS	EDUCATE ON IMPORTANCE OF RELAYING COMMUNICATION; POSITIVE ATTITUDE
STUDENTS	HIGH	LOW	AVOIDE CONFUSION; WHAT BUS TO TAKE	DIGEST COMMUNICATIONS	COMPLAIN	STRESS IMPORTANCE OF DIESTING THE UPCOMING COMMUNICATIONS; WHERE TO GO FOR MORE INFO
PARENTS	HIGH	HIGH	AVOIDE CONFUSION; WHAT BUS TO TAKE	DIGEST COMMUNICATIONS	COMPLAIN	STRESS IMPORTANCE OF DIESTING THE UPCOMING COMMUNICATIONS; WHERE TO GO FOR MORE INFO
PTA	LOW	HIGH	PUBLIC ACCEPTANCE; WORKABLE SOLUTION	ADVOCATE FOR ACCEPTANCE	NEGATIVE COMMUNICATIONS	EQUIP MEMBERS WITH PROJECT STATUS AND REASON FOR CHANGE

Figure20.4 – Complex Stakeholder Analysis Matrix

Regardless of the matrix type, each stakeholder is characterized by at a minimum- their level of *influence* of the change effort, and level of *impact* of its outcome.

By level of *influence*, I mean how much the stakeholder directly affects the direction, resources applied to the project, or can affect the perceived success of the project. If the people funding the change aren't happy with the way things are going, then your change effort will be at risk.

By level of *impact*, I mean to what degree the change alters people's professional or personal lives. A new financial accounting system will affect the budget manager quite a bit, while it may affect those workers in Human Resources very little.

INTERVIEWS (STEP 2)

In addition to Impact and Influence, other dimensions to consider are how the stakeholder wants to be associated with the change- Inform, Consult, Involve, Collaborate, Partner, Empower. When speaking with your stakeholder groups, be sure to capture how they want to be involved.

After you've identified each stakeholder group, interview them or otherwise assess ***what*** topics they prefer to know about, ***when*** they prefer to know about those topics, and ***how*** they prefer to be informed (i.e. what communications medium- emails, in person, written report, hallway posters, newsletters, social media, etc.).

During your interviews, determine their baseline understanding of the organizational change, and determine what questions, fears, and concerns they have about the change. You will use these later in designing your communications strategy to address these issues.

Remember to set strategic communications goals for your efforts. For example, a goal could be by the end of the stratcomm campaign, to have 80% of front-line workers who are 'sufficiently informed' of how the change will affect their work, as measured on a scale of 'uninformed', 'aware', 'sufficiently informed', and 'well informed'. Likewise, you could also assess the amount of adoption along the

Change Acceptance Curve above. You achieve these metrics through survey, sample interviews, or some other observed behavior or attitude change.

Communications Mediums (Step 3)

Figure out what the ways you could communicate with your stakeholders. Make a spreadsheet (or list) of the options available to you, and which will you use. Keep in mind, you'll need to match your available mediums to the mediums on which your stakeholders like to receive their news. Think about it, if people don't read their email, then maybe email is not the right choice for that group.

POSSIBLE COMMUNICATIONS MEDIUMS

Email Campaign	Social Media
Brochures	Web Site
Posters	Press Release
Town Hall Mtgs	Events
Videos	Marketing Collateral
PowerPoint	City Proclamations
Radio	Print
TV	Podcast

Figure 20.5 – Possible Communications Mediums

Authoring Messaging and Themes (Step 4)

Now that we know our stakeholders and their needs, and we also know what communications mediums are available, it's time to author messages for each of the stakeholder groups. In your message development, be sure to address these four topic areas.

- **Understanding** - When authoring your message, be sure to acknowledge their fears/concerns (shows you understand them)

- **Value** - Communicate the value of the organizational change (how life will be better);
- **Burning Platform** - explain what bad things will happen if the organization does not make these changes
- **Call to Action** - Make clear what the stakeholder is supposed to do now that they are informed

Develop a Communications Plan (Step 5)

Now that we know our stakeholders and their needs (from stakeholder analysis), and we also know what communications mediums are available, and we have identified knowledge needs for each of our stakeholder groups, it's time to integrate all four dimensions and create our stratcomm plan.

Stakeholder Group	Message Goal	Message Content	Message Medium	Message Schedule	How Measured?
School Board	Understand	Project description Project Timeline Understanding Value Burning Platform Call to Action	Email broadcast, town hall meeting, hall posters	1-Oct	Online survey October 7
Teachers	Training	Project description Project Timeline Understanding Value Burning Platform Call to Action	Town hall meeting	1-Oct	Online survey October 7
Students/Parents	Understand	Project description Project Timeline Understanding Value Burning Platform Call to Action	Email broadcast, press release	7-Oct	None
PTA	Understand	Project description Project Timeline Understanding Value Burning Platform Call to Action	Email broadcast, press release	7-Oct	None

Figure 20.5 – Sample StratComm Plan

The plan is basically an extension added onto the stakeholder analysis document. In the plan, you'll document - What stakeholder group you want to reach. What the message will be. What medium you will use to deliver it and when. Repeat this for each stakeholder group, and this becomes your communications plan. Now get to work!

For example, the following could be an initial message content, by email, to an entire department. It contains all the elements of a message content- change description, timeline, understanding, value, burning platform, call to action:

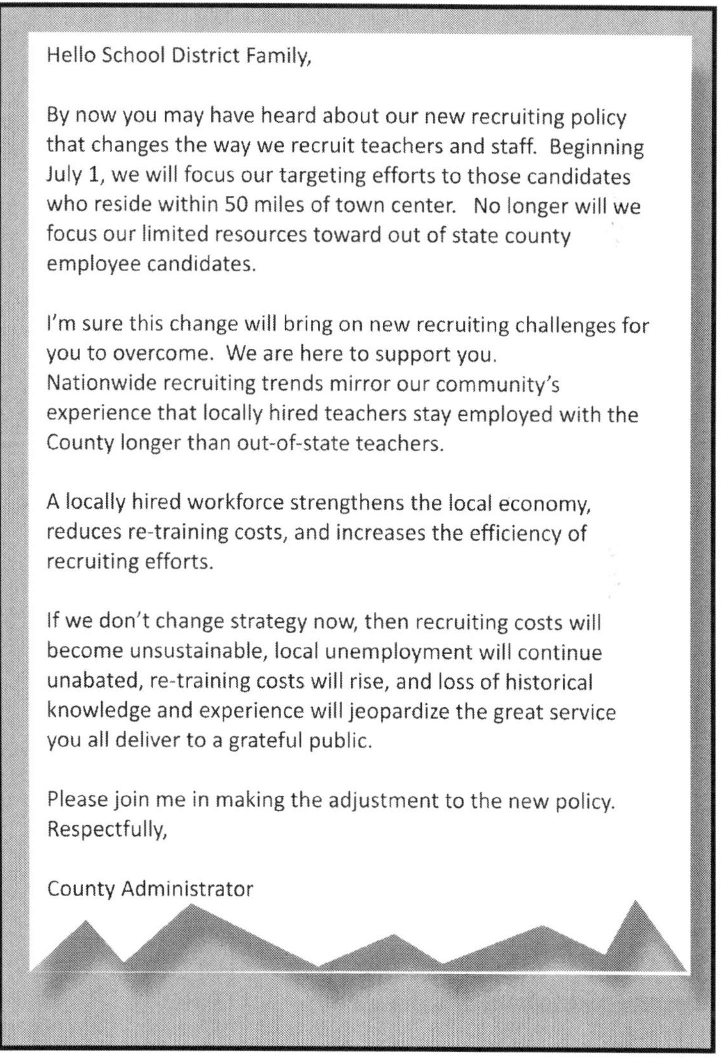

Hello School District Family,

By now you may have heard about our new recruiting policy that changes the way we recruit teachers and staff. Beginning July 1, we will focus our targeting efforts to those candidates who reside within 50 miles of town center. No longer will we focus our limited resources toward out of state county employee candidates.

I'm sure this change will bring on new recruiting challenges for you to overcome. We are here to support you. Nationwide recruiting trends mirror our community's experience that locally hired teachers stay employed with the County longer than out-of-state teachers.

A locally hired workforce strengthens the local economy, reduces re-training costs, and increases the efficiency of recruiting efforts.

If we don't change strategy now, then recruiting costs will become unsustainable, local unemployment will continue unabated, re-training costs will rise, and loss of historical knowledge and experience will jeopardize the great service you all deliver to a grateful public.

Please join me in making the adjustment to the new policy.
Respectfully,

County Administrator

Figure 20.6 – Sample Message Content

SMART TIPS

- Consider adding a graphic to serve as the logo (the branding) of your change. For Game of Thrones fans, this logo becomes your *sigil banner*! When people see your logo, they automatically know the topic that the communication refers to.
- Always add 'For more information' text to each communication piece, that points to a place the reader can get more information (set up web site, hotline, change champion).
- Before you deploy your communications message, test it against a small focus group before deploying it globally. This will help ensure that what you intended to communicate is actually received correctly.

MEASURING COMMUNICATIONS EFFECTIVENESS

How well did your communications strategies work? To measure the effectiveness of your strategic communications plan, you could measure any number of output items- press releases, email blasts, web site hits, town hall meetings, etc. However, if you recall from the goals chapter, it's better to measure *outcome*, not just *output*.

So, how do we measure outcome of a stratcomm plan? Answer- You measure how well people responded to your call to action, or how well the workers are informed and prepared for how the change will affect their work; or whatever your stratcomm goals are.

Normally, such outcome-based stratcomm evaluations are qualitative (personal feelings), and you measure, through a worker survey where your stakeholders are on the change curve *Awareness, Understanding, Engagement, Acceptance, Commitment, Internalization* (using in person, online, paper-based, focus group, whatever),–.

Be sure to communicate how you will use the results of the survey, and where participants can go see the results.

If you develop questions, then develop an even number of possible responses (4 or 6) for each question. In this way you force the respondent to make a choice either slanted in the positive or negative direction; and prevent a middle of the road response (which is of little value).

I've always been annoyed by survey designers who craft questions, for responses that add little value. For example, what year did Columbus sail the ocean blue? Of course the answer is 1492 but what does knowing the year matter? What if it was 1493? Better survey questions ask the reader to respond in a way that gauges the readers' understanding. For example, a better question to ask is- "What was the impact of Columbus reaching the Americas?"

Possible Responses:

a) It "opened" the New World to exploration and to conquest
b) Columbus's coming signaled doom for native societies
c) Europeans took millions of people from Africa to work as slaves in the New World

Similarly, craft survey questions that allow you to gauge understanding. For example,

MARGINAL QUESTION: Do you know where to go for more information about the organizational change?

- *Very Much*
- *Mostly*
- *Somewhat*
- *Not really*

Okay, where *do* they go? The responses this question doesn't tell us much.

BETTER QUESTION: Select all responses for where to go for more information about the organizational change?

- *Supervisor*
- *Intranet*

- *Email broadcasts*
- *I don't know where to go*

This question and response set tells us much more about the respondents' understanding.

Also, include an opportunity for the participant to submit comments about your project. This will help you receive information that you hadn't asked about, and it gives the worker an opportunity to vent frustrations or ask questions (which will help in your next communications piece).

Here are sample survey questions to measure the effectiveness of your organizational change. What ways can you make these questions more informative and meaningful?

Because of agency communication strategies, how well prepared do you feel to perform your job?

- *Fully prepared*
- *Prepared*
- *Somewhat Prepared*
- *Unprepared*

How much of a typical company newsletter do you read?

- *Read most of it*
- *Read some of it*
- *Only skim through it*
- *Don't read it at all*

From which of the following sources do you now receive most of your information about what is going on in the department? Rank your top three information sources only.

- *Director Emails to workforce*
- *My supervisor*
- *Company leadership*
- *Group meetings at our work location*
- *Company intranet*

- *Company e-mail*
- *Hall Posters*
- *Social Media sites*

Which of the following best describes your impression of communications at <company>?

- *Keeps me fully informed*
- *Keeps me fairly informed*
- *Gives me only a limited amount of information*
- *Gives me no amount of information*

How useful do you find the information you currently receive?

- *Very useful*
- *Somewhat useful*
- *Not very useful*
- *Not useful at all*

How would you rate your knowledge of the company; its strategic direction, policies, ongoing accomplishments and the issues facing the company?

(1 'not knowledgeable to 5 'highly knowledgeable')

- *Strategic Direction 1 2 3 4 5*
- *Policies and Procedures 1 2 3 4 5*
- *Ongoing Accomplishments 1 2 3 4 5*
- *Issues facing the University 1 2 3 4 5*

From the following topics, which ones do you believe are vital you receive communication about? (Choose as many as you like)

- *Topic 1*
- *Topic 2*
- *Topic 3*

What are the circumstances if your business unit does not change?

- *Improved Capability*
- *No Change*
- *Degraded Capability*

How does your business unit help meet the program's goals and objectives?

- *Critical Contribution*
- *Significant Contribution*
- *Minor Contribution*
- *No Contribution*

How well does your immediate supervisor inspire you to support the organizational change?

- *Very Much*
- *Mostly*
- *Somewhat*
- *Not really*

Do you know where to go for more information about the organizational change?

- *Very Much*
- *Mostly*
- *Somewhat*
- *Not really*

Words to grow by:

- Change Champion – an early adopter who supports your organizational change and acts as a facilitator to its success.

NOW YOU TRY IT!

Think about a current or upcoming project. Which group of stakeholders will be your 'early adopters'?

____

____

____

Name one internal stakeholder group and one external stakeholder group. What is their level of impact (hi/lo); what is their level of influence (hi/lo)?

____

____

____

____

____

List five communications mediums available to you.

-
-
-
-
-

For one of your stakeholder groups, give one bullet point for how life will be better for them, after the change.

____

____

____

____

Describe what will happen if the change does not occur (the burning platform).

____

____

____

____

PART III

CAPSTONE PROJECT

Organizational Assessment

Chapter 21

Whether you're leading a new organization or just need to re-invigorate your existing one, an organizational assessment is a proven method for discovering the good, the bad, and the ugly of your business unit- as seen from the perspective of those closest to the work (like a car mechanic conducting a thorough vehicle inspection).

Objectives	**Terms**
When you complete Chapter 21, you will be able to: • Describe two techniques to select the optimal solution, from among competing solutions	• Findings Document • As-Is State • To-Be State

In simple terms, an organizational assessment is a structured interview and analysis process that results in a *Findings Document.* The findings document describes the status (the good, the bad, the ugly) of what your organization does, and how well it works, and what needs to be fixed… from the perspective of those closest to the work.

I say 'from the perspective of those closest to the work' because what you're really after here is to discover gaps between what management perceives to be true, and what the workforce perceives to be true. For example, if management perceives that workers are conducting quality checks on their work product; but in reality, no quality checks occur because the only way workers can keep up with the high volume of work is to forgo the quality checks, but sign off as if they actually did them. This disconnect is what you hope to discover, so you can take corrective action.

Avoid the temptation to become discouraged or insecure, and not be able to "handle the truth", unlike the emperor in the fairytale -'The Emperor's New Clothes' who didn't want to accept the truth. Don't fall for this trap. You WANT to find where your perception and understanding differ from these closest to the work. Discovering the gap is the most valuable piece of information that you're after. The successful TV series "Undercover Boss" is based on this premise; as the boss discovers valuable information vital to the survival of his company.

For this example, the organizational assessment will be a Workload Organizational Assessment. It will reveal what work the team performs. How well they perform it. What issues they face. What problems and inefficiencies exist; and answers many more questions. Again, from the perspective of those closest to the work.

You use interviews to speak with different team members and ask a pre-set series of questions to gather factual data, and to determine the workers perspective of the 'current-state', also known as 'as-is state', of their particular work unit. When conducting the interview, take notes, and draw pictures, and process maps as needed. Then later compile them into electronic format.

FINDINGS DOCUMENT

In the strategic planning stage, you will analyze this findings document to determine if the worker's perceptions are valid, and then make a strategy to close both the reality gap, and the perception gap.

ORGANIZATIONAL ASSESSMENT DOCUMENT

INTRODUCTION
- PROJECT PLAN HIGHLIGHTS
- DELIVERABLES
- RISKS/ASSUMPTIONS/CONSTRAINTS

KEY FINDINGS
ASSESSMENT METHODOLOGY
DATA COLLECTION INTERVIEW
- DIAGNOSTIC QUESTIONS

FINDINGS, OBSERVATIONS, RECOMMENDATIONS
NEXT STEPS

Figure 21.1 – Organizational Assessment Format

The assessment findings document can take on various formats, but here's one we'll work with that's proven to be effective. Below is a sample outline with section headings.

Introduction Section

Describes the reason for the assessment, high level project plan, deliverables, risks, constraints, and assumptions.

Key Findings Section

Describes the discovered themes that seem to affect all business units assessed.

Assessment Methodology Section

Describes how the assessment was conducted. Usually, through interviews, research, data collection, sample products, etc.

Data Collection Interview Section

Where you ask the pre-defined questions, and collect the responses. This section usually contains your paragraph descriptions, tables of information, and graphs. Topics covered can be business unit description, staffing model description, work schedules, work throughput measures, or any other topic of interest.

Your assessment could ask the below questions (and follow-up questions) as part of your Root Cause analysis (RCA):

- Describe the people on you team- how many, where are they, and what do they do?
- Average number of widgets produced per month/week/day?
- Highlight key challenges inhibiting their performance?
- How many hours of job-specific training/education have they had in last two fiscal years?
- How do they define success in their work?
- What are their performance targets in their unit? How well are they meeting those targets?
- What should the performance targets be for the unit?
- Do they have the necessary amount of authority to perform their job? What authority could improve their performance/results?
- What efficiencies do they think could be applied to their job tasks?
- If more resources were added to you unit, what services would they like to provide that they don't provide now?
- What technologies could enhance their success and productivity?
- Characterize how their work hours vary (preferred scheduling)
- What other considerations should be included, that haven't been asked?

Findings/Observations/Recommendations Section

Describes the findings from the data that was collected. It describes (with data proof) what works well, and what needs to be fixed. This is the really juicy and valuable part of the assessment. It's the fruit that all the previous work was all for. It describes key challenges inhibiting performance, performance targets, performance bottlenecks, efficiency opportunities, decision-making authorities, and all the answers that the Power Leader needs to know to move the organization forward.

All of the information in this section becomes the input to the strategic plan coming up in the next phase.

Next Steps Section

Describes the next activity required to fulfill the recommendations of this document. A next step could be to present your findings; or receive the boss's permission to continue, or perhaps reward good performance, or strategize to fix the parts not going well.

Example Assessment

The below is an example response from a government agency's Payroll section.

Start with developing a questions list that is relevant to your organization. These probing questions should open the door for you to discover the 'things you want to know' (see example questions above). Then schedule and conduct interviews with a subject matter expert for that business unit, usually the supervisor.

Create Investigative Questions

For example, Question: How many workers are in the unit (full-time and part-time)? What are their work schedules and locations?

- *2 employees at 37.5hrs/week each, this equals a maximum of 75 possible man-hours of work per week*
- *Processing 670 time sheets every other week, the bi-weekly workload cycles between heavy and light*

Cluster Work Activity

Question: Cluster all your work into 5 groups, and approximate the weekly (or monthly) percent of time working those activities? Elicit 4-5 work activities for each work cluster.

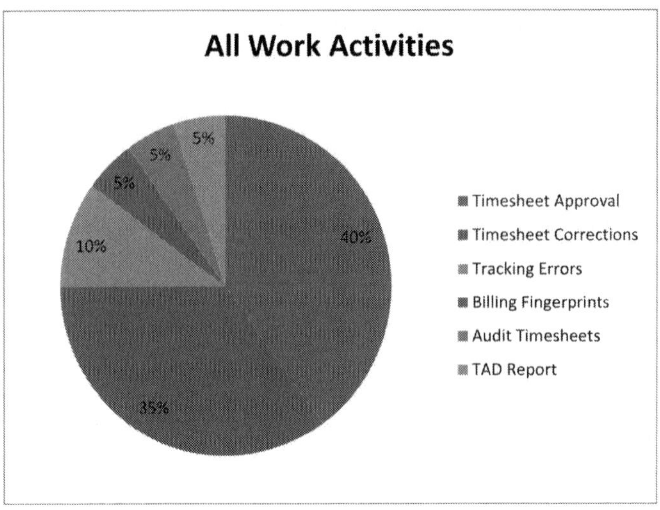

Figure 21.2 – Cluster of All Work Activities

Activity Category	*Sub-task*	*% Time Commitment*
Timesheet Approval	*Manually sum hours*	*40%*
	Review for compliance	
	Approve timesheet	
Timesheet Corrections	*Contact employee*	*35%*
	Investigate error	
	Resubmit timesheet	
Tracking Errors	*Log error*	*10%*
	Analyze errors	
	Report on errors	
Billing Fingerprints	*Sum hours*	*5%*
	Create invoice	
	Mail invoice	
Audit Timesheets	*Collect samples*	*5%*
	Analyze results	
	Write findings	
TAD Report	*Sum hours*	*5%*
	Write report	
	Submit report	

Table – 21.1 - Work Activities for each Cluster

Notice the majority of time is spent to review and approve submitted time sheets (40%). What's more interesting is that another majority (35%) is spent correcting incorrect time sheets. This finding would likely make its way into the section describing *key findings*. If you recall, it's more efficient and less costly to prevent problems than to have to fix them. Therefore, investigating reasons for time sheet corrections is a ripe candidate for further efficiency and waste research.

Be mindful that some employees may come up with over 100%. You'll need to determine if they over/under estimated the time required to complete some activity, or if they truly work beyond their normal work schedule. I've seen cases where the employee routinely works beyond their work schedule to keep up with the workload but never claim the extra time on her time card. This is bad for several reasons: 1) she cheats herself out of compensation; 2) it gives her boss a false understanding of the true time it takes to complete a task; and 3) sets up for failure the next person who takes over her role.

Work Throughput

Now that you have clustered work activity into manageable quantities, dive down further and ask *work throughput* questions-meaning how much time it takes to process one unit of work (ex. review and approve a single timesheet).

Question: What is the average time to process 1 timesheet? What is the average time to process all 670 timesheets?

Worker response: *Timesheets fall into easy, intermediate, and difficult. It takes just over one week each for two employees to accomplish all 670 timesheets*

REVIEW & APPROVE			
Difficulty 760 Timesheets	**% of Timesheets**	**Process Time**	**Duration**
Easy	15%	3 min	15% x 760 x 3 = ~5.75 hrs
Intermediate	70%	4-6 min 5 min Avg	70% x 760 x 5 = ~44.5 hrs
Difficult	15%	10-20 min 15 minAvg	15% x 760 x 15 = ~28.5 hrs
			78.75 man-hours

Table 21.2 - Work Throughput for Review & Approve Process

Question: Average time to process corrections?

Worker Response: *Approximately 11 man-hours each per week for the two employees to accomplish.*

(670 @ +/- 15% error rate = average of 100 to be corrected)

CORRECTIONS			
Difficulty 114 Timesheets Avg	**% of Timesheets**	**Process Time**	**Duration**
Easy	15%	5 min	15% x 114 x 5 = 1.5 hrs
Intermediate	70%	10-14 min 12 min Avg	70% x 114 x 12 = 16 hrs
Difficult	15%	10-40 min 20 min Avg	15% x 114 x 20 = 5.75 hrs
			23.25 man-hrs

Table 21.3 - Work Throughput for Corrections

Question: How many man-hours does it take to process an audit?

Worker Response: *Timesheet audit involves reviewing approximately 50 timesheets per payroll submission (every other week).*

AUDIT			
Difficulty 50 Timesheets	**% of Timesheets**	**Process Time**	**Duration**
Easy	15%	3 min	15% x 50 x 3 = 0.5 hrs
Intermediate	70%	4-6 min 5 min Avg	70% x 50 x 5 = 8.75 hrs
Difficult	15%	10-20 min 15 min Avg	15% x 50 x 15 = 5.75 hrs
			15.0 man-hrs

Table 21.4 - Work Throughput for Audit

Question: How long does it take to perform fingerprint billing?

Worker Response: *Fingerprint billing occurs month for 6 agencies. Each billing effort takes 60 minutes each, yielding an average of approximately 6 man-hours per month.*

Question: How long does it take to create and deliver the Turnaround document?

Worker Response: *Turn Around Document (TAD) report is due every other week and takes approximately 1.5-2 hours to create.*

ADDITIONAL ACTIVITIES			
Activity	**Process Time**	**Monthly Quantity**	**Duration**
Fingerprint Billing	2.5 man-hours	4 per month	2.5 x 4 = 10 man-hours
RFIs	.25 man hours	40 per month	.25 x 40 = 10 man-hours
Turnaround Report	1.5 man-hours	2 per month	3 x 2 = 3 man-hours
			23 man-hrs per month
			5.75 man-hours per week

Table 21.5 - Work Throughput for Additional Activities

In summary, the two clerks combined work throughput for the two week period consumes 122.75 hours (78.75 + 23.25 + 15 + 5.75), of the 150 available man-hours; leaving 27.25 hours extra time. That's 14.6 hours each remaining for the two employees.

Think about this: How do the workers account for the unaccounted 27.25 man-hours?! What do they do with this *free* time? Are the time estimates wrong? What does this tell you? Should you hire more Payroll staff? If so, how many and when?

Now that you've committed to your answer on how many you should hire and when, I'm guessing you probably said "I don't need to hire any more clerks because we have enough to do all the work. In fact, the workers have 27.25 hours extra! Ha! Gotcha! Keep in mind that we didn't take into account for meetings, random tasks, bathroom breaks, or most importantly for a *relief factor*.

Relief Factor

A relief factor is a number (usually 1.3 to 1.7) that indicates how many extra workers you need to have to perform one (1) job. On average across all industries, these combined non-productive activities consume approximately 0.3-0.7 of an employee's available time to do work and produce output. While the payroll workload consumes almost 100% of two full-time worker's time, we didn't account for non-work activities that take away from workers reviewing and approving timesheets - sick time, vacation time, training, company meetings, bathroom breaks, interruptions, etc. Therefore, we only really get 77% of output producing work from each employee!

So, really, the total available man-hours to do payroll processing is not 150 as stated earlier, but actually only 115.5 available man-hours (77% x 150). This means that your two payroll clerks are somehow fitting in an extra 7.25 man-hours (122.75 – 115.5) every two weeks. How do they do this? Do they consume overtime? Are they not taking vacation? Are they working when sick? Do they never get training? Do they never get bathroom breaks? Are they working extra but not reporting the hours? Or worse, are they somehow doing something that reduces the work quality or maybe cheating (approving reports without checking them), so they can fit in all the work there is to do?

Another way to look at it is to hire one part-time payroll worker to supplement the existing two clerks (2 clerks x 1.3 relief factor = 2.6 clerks).

But given that the process of approving timesheets IS a defacto audit. Before you hire a part time clerk, what if you eliminated the extra 15 man-hour Audit task (and thus improve efficiency)? Then you could reduce the actual workload by 15 man-hours available for the Payroll team to meet the relief factor...with a little left over for a bathroom break ☺

Uncover Roadblocks

Question: Highlight Key challenges inhibiting your performance?

- When an employee makes an error, sending the employee instructions for fixing themselves it are only 50% effective
- Audits are being conducted as a natural part of the corrections process, and could be eliminated as a work task
- Workers don't check their time cards for the easy/simple errors. Causes increased workload on the back end in corrections
- Inconsistent application of timekeeping rules between supervisors and Divisions. Payroll has recommended a timekeeping policy manual
- The location of Payroll section is in a high-traffic area and can be distracting as employees walk past or hold discussions with the Budget office in the same area. However, Payroll employees do not want to move office location
- The timekeeping software (web-based) is slow to respond

Question: What efficiencies do you think could be applied to your job tasks?

- To link Timekeeping software with Staff Scheduling software so they can share information.

- Better reporting capability in timesheet software
- Faster network response from timekeeping software. Experiencing significant network delay.
- Employees submit timesheets on time, thus eliminating the need to 'back-check' and send reminder emails
- Ability for payroll software to direct message the sender within the software application
- Obtaining a list of employees and their current supervisor. (shift roster)

Question: If more resources were added to your unit, what services would you like to provide that you don't provide now?

- Outreach efforts to train new employees
- More and better analytical reporting (overtime consumption, trends, patterns)

Question: What technologies could enhance your success and productivity?

- Integrating multiple agency software systems
- Better reporting solution/ability
- Faster response from payroll software
- Automated Error Checking before submission

Question: Characterize how your work hours vary (preferred scheduling)

- 37.5hrs per week

Other Investigatory Questions

Question: How many hours of job-specific training/education have you had in last two fiscal years?

- Payroll software (4-5hrs), Budgeting software (4hrs), CPR (2 hrs) one time only
- Would like to have training and education in taxes, withholdings, and Excel spreadsheet

Question: How do you define success in your work?

- Complete review and approval of all timesheets on time
- Feel accomplished when delivers correct/accurate/timely timesheets
- Develop positive relationships with other employees

Question: What are your performance targets in your unit? How well are you meeting those targets?

- To meet processing deadline 100% of the time. Currently meeting 100% of goal
- Goal of 5% error rate. Closest they came was 6%. On average experiencing 15% error rate.

Question: What should your performance targets be for your unit?

- Goal of 5% error rate.

Question: Do you have the necessary amount of authority to perform your job? What authority could improve your performance/results?

- Yes. We have sufficient authority to perform our jobs and communicate with others

Question: What other considerations should be included, that haven't been asked?

- None

FINDINGS, OBSERVATIONS, RECOMMENDATIONS

Now, review the collected responses and supporting data, and analyze them for opportunities to improve. As you do, consider four dimensions- People, Process, Technology, and Physical Infrastructure. Capture these findings, observations, and recommendations in the findings document. These will later become goals and strategies.

The following organizational assessment snippet (Table 21.6) presents a small portion of an entire organizational assessment findings document (Figure 21.1). Now, repeat this assessment interview for each of your business units. Combine all findings into a single document. Voila! The findings in this document are the goals of the upcoming Strategic Plan, coming up next.

Tip! If your business unit has lost focus or you want to reinvigorate it, then conduct an organizational assessment and receive a fresh new look at what's going on.

	Dimension	Payroll Unit Findings, Observations, Recommendations
1	People	Possible need to hire 1 part time clerk. There is no existing relief factor applied to work. Workers unable to take training, and frequently lose earned vacation time during year carry-over.
2	Process	The task of timesheet audit (of 50 timesheets) per payroll submission (every other week) could be eliminated because the audit is already being accomplished through the process of correcting timesheets. A potential savings of 7.5 man-hours per week. May not be sufficient to alleviate the need for the proposed part-time clerk.
3	People	Inconsistent application of timekeeping rules between supervisors and Divisions. Payroll has recommended developing a timekeeping policy manual.
4	Process	To enhance accountability for error-checking, consider adding correct timesheets as part of employee PFP.
5	People	Employees request training in Excel software
6	Technology	Obtain a spreadsheet of employees and their current supervisor (shift roster)
7	Infrastructure	Rearrange the cubicles to block the discussion noise. Consider raising the cubicle height.

Table 21.6 – Findings, Observations, Recommendations

BONUS CHAPTER
Your First 30 Days

Chapter 22

You want to be successful, lead your team on its mission, and impress those around you. I'm sure you are both excited and fearful of what is to come. Not to worry, this chapter will guide you along a proven four phase model, so you can take on your new role with confidence.

Objectives	**Terms**
When you complete Chapter 22, you will be able to: • Describe three key activities to enact within your first 30 days of taking command	• Buy-In • Define • Discover • Plan • Execute

SHOW QUICK WINS

As a Power Leader, you need to let your boss and team members know you were the right choice to lead. You must show quick wins now! Your selection of wins should come from two groups:

- Solve concerns identified by your boss, and
- Solve concerns identified by your team members

By addressing both key stakeholder groups, you build support and confidence from the groups closest to your professional survival. With support from both of these groups, you can accomplish anything!

Begin with simple or cosmetic fixes. These are easy, quick wins that show you can actually change things for the better. Simple and cosmetic fixes are the first step in gaining buy-in and trust from both your boss and co-workers. For example, I'm thinking of a Power Leader who successfully made a simple fix to resolve the difficulty of finding a replacement worker for a shift that's short staffed. The Power Leader allowed his supervisors to pre-identify and pre-schedule a stand-by replacement worker, in case a regularly scheduled worker called in sick. This simple solution eliminated the last minute scramble to find a worker to come in to work; and avoided employee anger when unexpectedly forced to report to work on a day off. A simple and quick win!

Other quick wins, for example, could be your commitment to deliver the weekly performance report to the boss BEFORE she asks for it; or re-shuffling job duties to take over an annoying work task from your boss, so he can focus on other matters; or painting the office walls; or best yet- allow jeans on Fridays, or authorize workers to work from home one day a week. These small wins, for both the boss and workers, build momentum and trust needed to achieve the bigger and more meaningful wins later.

Create Employee Buy-In

As the new leader, you will need sustained employee buy-in to successfully transform your organization from where it is, to where you want it to be (Organizational Transformation). Simply forcing change on people will not work. You can achieve employee buy-in and compliance through a number of ways. So let's talk about sticks and carrots.

Measure and Reward what You Care About

In addition to mission progress, make a deliberate effort to also measure worker compliance to organizational values.

For example, when an agency says they value truthfulness but does nothing to reward or discipline workers' adherence to the value, then unhealthy organizational culture develops, and performance drops.

Awards and Accolades

Frequently, supervisors overlook and don't take advantage of putting their workers in for awards and accolades. A great way to build trust and momentum is to submit your workers for departmental awards and recognition. Your nominations engender support and buy-in, especially early on, for your organizational change.

Drive Organizational Culture

A team will often take on the personality of its leader. If the leader is sloppy, then that communicates a message and culture of 'sloppiness'. Similarly, if the leader values innovation, then a culture of innovation will grow. Here's how you can create a supportive organizational culture.

- Launch a strong strategic communications effort to educate workers on corporate values, and communicate that worker adherence to the values will be measured and rewarded (and disciplined, it goes without saying)
- Add a performance component to each worker's annual performance assessment criteria. In general, workers will perform according to what is *actually* rewarded or disciplined, rather than what behaviors that executives *suggest* should happen. So ensure the behavior you want to happen is tied to a reward and discipline system

- Tie worker performance to an operational benefit, such as first choice in shift selection, first choice in office/cube selection, or a highly sought after training class, etc.
- Create an annual award for the top performers for both performance, and a separate award for adherence to organizational values (the NFL does this with the Walter Peyton award). Include issuing a trophy or plaque, and include bonus $, vacation days, conference trip, etc. where possible.

YOUR FIRST STEPS

For this case study, let's assume, you've been promoted, transferred, or assigned to lead a new government project or program. Starting the first day in you new assignment (after you get a good cup of coffee), your 30-day management goals should be:

- WEEK 1 (Define) Meet with your boss. Understand your mission. Meet with your staff and tell them to expect change.
- WEEK 2 (Discover) Assess your organizations strengths, weaknesses, opportunities, and threats through an organizational assessment.
- WEEK 3 (Plan) Develop organizational goals, and a strategic plan to achieve those goals
- WEEK 4 (Execute) Launch and execute the strategic plan; monitor progress and control for quality; make time for the tea and medals to follow.

Let's use our phased approach structure to help us get a handle on our plan. I'm not presenting the *leadership* things you're gonna do (that's a different topic), but instead, I propose the *management* things you're gonna do - Define, Discover, Plan, and Execute.

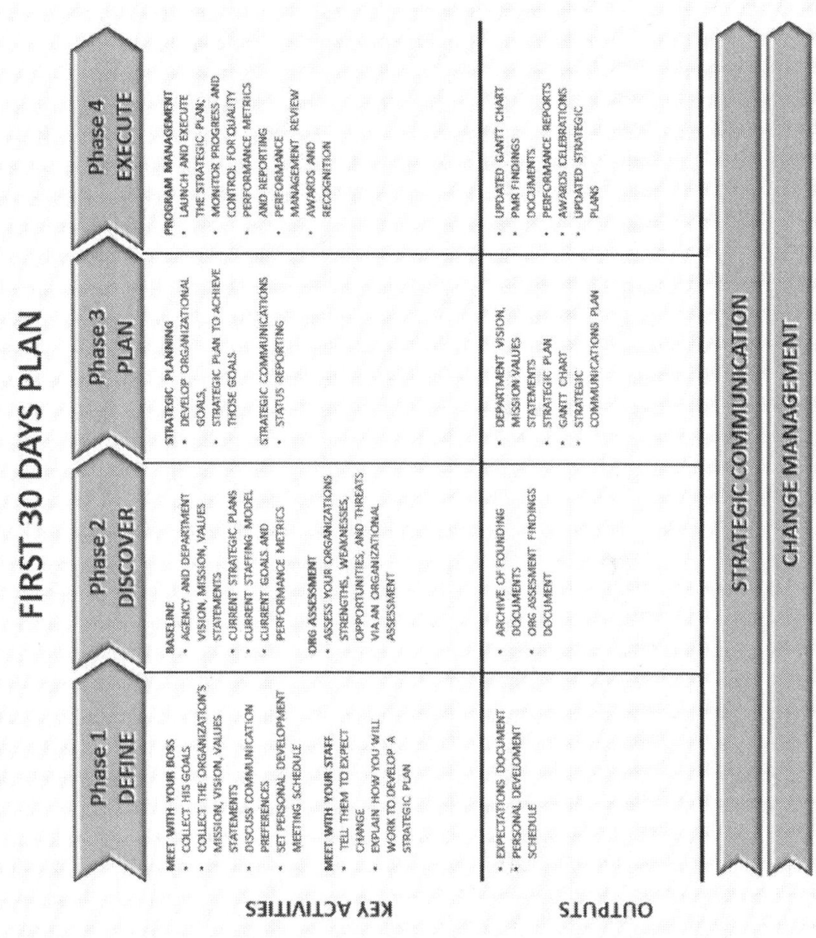

Figure 22.1 – 4 Phased Model Approach

DEFINE

Phase one – Meet with your boss and understand his expectations of you, and his goals for your business unit. (See chapter What Does the Boss Expect; and See chapter on SMART goals.) Discuss how he prefers to communicate (in person, email, memos, forms, formal reports, etc.), and how often. Identify what issues he prefers to be consulted on and which issues you can manage yourself.

- Sometimes getting regular contact with your boss is difficult to schedule, or is just plain awkward. To overcome this difficulty and lay the groundwork for strong communication, during this expectations discussion, see if your boss will agree to schedule regular recurring one-on-one meeting with you. This will create regular opportunities to discuss program issues, and especially to discuss your career development.
- After your expectations discussion, refresh yourself with the agency Vision, Mission, and Values statements, and your particular business unit vision, mission, and values statements. If there isn't a separate set of statements for your business unit, then work with your team to create them. (See chapter on Vision, Mission, and Values Statements). Ensure they align with and support the agency statements.
- Next, meet with your staff, either one-on-one, or in larger groups. Introduce yourself and let them know that you've met with your boss and have discussed plans for the future. That you want to meet with them to gather their insight. You don't need to discuss what any plans are, but **be sure to tell your workers to expect change**. Preparing your staff for change, and engaging them in the change process is the first step in change management (see chapter on Change Management)

DISCOVER

Phase two - It's time to figure out the current state of your program or project, so you can have a solid foundation from which to build a strategy moving forward. You obtain current-state information through an *organizational assessment.* (See chapter on Organizational Assessment, and chapter on Performance Metrics) that assesses your organizations strengths, weaknesses, opportunities, and threats (see chapter on SWOT).

This Discover phase is where you also launch your strategic communications plan as part of your larger organizational change effort. (See chapter on Change Management, and chapter on Strategic Communications) Please note that strategic communications and change management begin very early in your projects and continue throughout the change effort. The theme of your first communication is to communicate that change is coming, you will assess the good/bad/ugly, and their cooperation and support will be vital. This sets the expectation of workers' participation and support in the process.

The info uncovered during the assessment will be used to create you *Strategic Plan* (see chapter on Strategic Planning). Got it? Let me repeat. Organizational Assessment leads to the Strategic Plan. See how the management concepts and skills fit together?

ORGANIZATIONAL ASSESSMENT LEADS TO THE STRATEGIC PLAN

During the organizational assessment you want to find out what work the team performs. How well they perform it, and their performance metrics. What issues they face. What problems and inefficiencies exist, and answers to many more questions. You'll use interviews to speak with different subject matter expert team members and ask a series of questions to determine the program 'current-state', also known as 'as-is state', of their particular work responsibility.

From the organizational assessment, you will create a findings document that describes your assessment findings, observations, and recommendations. This document is the rich and refined information source that will drive your strategic planning efforts! You will transform these findings, observation and recommendations into organizational goals and strategies.

PLAN

Gather your leadership team, and come to a shared understanding and agreement that it's possible that what they all think is happening may not *actually* be ground truth; that they should open their minds to a difference between what you all think should be happening, may not be what is actually happening. Discuss the findings document and make a commitment to close the gap between perception and reality.

From the assessment findings document, work with your team to develop a strategic plan that includes goals, metrics, and strategies. (See chapter on Strategic Planning). Be sure to include your boss's expectations, and your personal goals for your business unit.

EXECUTE

Now it's time to focus on the remaining 50% of program and project management, and that's implementing your strategies and monitoring and controlling their effectiveness and progress.

Performance Metrics and Reporting
The program is off and running, and now it's time to monitor how your strategy is progressing. You'll want to assess your strategy performance by reviewing your previously identified performance and quality metrics (see chapter on Performance Metrics). You should deliver and receive regular performance reporting. Compare the organization's performance to the goals to see how well you're doing. As needed, alter your strategy to improve your performance.

Performance Management Review (PMR)
Pay attention, to this. On a regular basis, perhaps monthly, you should sponsor and hold performance management review sessions. (See chapter on PMR). During these sessions have your team present their SWOT charts and other performance measures (see chapter on SWOT). During the PMRs, it's a great time to offer rewards and other forms of motivation.

Strategic Communications
Underlining the entire program management process should be a strong strategic communications program. Use it as an opportunity to celebrate your successes, communicate your progress, and keep the momentum going. Employee morale also hinges upon strategic communications, so they are reminded

that they are part of something bigger than themselves, and their time and efforts are worth it.

THAT'S IT!

The only thing left is for you to host or attend the in-person seminar "Management Essentials for Rising Leaders". There, you'll have more in-depth explanation and guided hands-on learning, using *your* specific challenges for your case studies!

Visit www.beapowerleader.com for more information

Now go do good work!

You're still reading?

About the Author

Charles "Chuck" Manning is the founder of Spark Management Consulting, a government-focused consulting firm based out of the Washington, D.C. metropolitan area.

His 30 year career spans both the public and private sectors- serving as a local government official; as a private sector management consultant with a global management consulting firm; and as a contributing team member to a successful, two-term political campaign strategy team.

He applies his local, national, and international executive management experience to help government organizations, large and small, solve their toughest challenges and transform them to a higher level of performance. His clients have included the Federal Bureau of Investigation (FBI), U.S. Drug Enforcement Administration (DEA), Central Intelligence Agency (CIA), Immigration and Customs Enforcement (ICE), Naval Criminal Investigative Service (NCIS), U.S. Military, national government of Afghanistan, and U.S. local governments.

He holds a Master's degree in Public Administration and is a certified Project Management Professional (PMP).

Made in the USA
Middletown, DE
30 July 2018